D1626657

993400475 5
Withdrawn

# HOLIDAYS FROM THE PAST

PAUL ATTERBURY

**NO VACANCIES**

HOLIDAYS

"KISS ME ON MY UPPER LIP BECAUSE MY BOTTOM'S SORE!"

*Splendid choice*

Butlins-

Minehead-

British Railways-

and you

# HOLIDAYS FROM THE PAST

## A treasure trove of holiday memories

PAUL ATTERBURY

FIRENZE
GRAND HÔTEL

WAITRESS
SERVICE ➔

Published by AA Publishing, a trading name of AA Media Limited, whose registered office is Fanum House, Basing View, Basingstoke, Hampshire RG21 4EA. Registered number 06112600.

Packaged for AA Media Limited by OutHouse!, Shalbourne, Marlborough SN8 3QJ

For OutHouse!:
Managing Editor  Sue Gordon
Art Editor  Dawn Terrey

For AA Publishing:
Internal Repro  Sarah Montgomery
Production  Stephanie Allen

Cover  Louise Turpin

First published in the UK in 2008 as *On Holiday*
Reprinted 2008
This edition published 2011

A CIP catalogue record for this book is available from the British Library.

ISBN 978-0-7495-7157-3

Printed in China by C&C Offset Printing Co., Ltd

A04702

# CONTENTS

CHEERIO!—I'M OFF FOR MY HOLIDAY!

HOLIDAYS IN HOLLAND

Conducted inclusive tours to
Charming Holland

Organised by Netherlands Railways (1963)

# THE HOLIDAY TRADITION

# GETTING AWAY FROM IT ALL

As a nation we have been holidaying for over 200 years. Initially visits to the seaside, the country, the mountains or to spa towns were made in pursuit of health and a fashionable life. Such trips were expensive and exclusive, and it was not until the Victorians began to change the face of Britain that holidays became more universal. The rapidly spreading railway network enabled everyone to travel more easily, and cheaply, and this in turn encouraged the development of resorts. Indeed, many of the most famous holiday regions in Britain were created by the railways and their associated shipping lines. A further impetus was the Bank Holiday Act of 1871, and by the early 1900s paid holiday time was a well-established concept. A day by the sea soon became a week's holiday. By the 1920s and 1930s the holiday experience was enjoyed by all, along with the defining features that helped to make it memorable: the hotels, boarding houses and holiday camps, the restaurants and cafés, the beach and its related entertainments, the piers and theatres, the clothes and holiday paraphernalia, the souvenirs. Going on holiday became a ritual at the very core of our culture.

△ In the 1920s and 1930s guests were regularly photographed outside their boarding house as a way of commemorating their holiday. This group of people, who had probably never met before their holiday, reveals an interesting variety of dress styles.

SECTION OF THE COLOURFUL GARDENS AND LAWNS AT BUTLIN'S          GV 9

△ The holiday camp was for many people their first holiday experience. Butlin's was the market leader, and this card shows the diverse and colourful life offered in its camps.

△ Until the 1960s camping was universally popular. Standards were maintained, as indicated by this photograph of a tea party, complete with tablecloth and tea cosy.

A Splendid Motor Run from Glasgow

Or Travel via BALLOCH (L.N.E.R. or L.M.S.) or
via CRAIGENDORAN and WEST HIGHLAND
RAILWAY to ARROCHAR & TARBET Station

The Tarbet Hotel
• LOCH LOMOND •

MOUNTAINEERING
TROUT AND SALMON
FISHING · BOATING
TENNIS
SPLENDID ROADS FOR
MOTORING & CYCLING

Principal Hotel on the Loch — in the
Centre of the Grandest Highland Scenery

△ This decorative card promoted a famous Scottish hotel.
The writer, in February 1936, enjoyed 'a splendid hot
lunch with a roaring fire' before a walk by Loch Lomond.

◁ This is Joan at Mablethorpe, wearing a rather exotic
beach dress and a very glamorous hat.

△ Dorothy, in Fulham, was sent this card in 1924 by her
mother, who perhaps is the somewhat overdressed lady in
the centre of the picture. The chalet was in Sussex.

This book is about the typical holiday experience. It is about memories, a vision of the family lives that we all had, or would like to think we had. At its heart is that great but largely overlooked document of social history, the amateur family photograph. We have been taking photographs of ourselves on holiday since the Edwardian era, and before that other people, usually more professional, took them for us. Postcards and brochures also document our holiday experiences, and it is the combination of all these things that forms the basis for this book. It is arranged in sections that explore visually where we stayed, what we wore, where we went, how we travelled and what we did.

Throughout the period covered by the book, roughly from the Edwardians to the 1970s, the British went on holiday in Britain. We went primarily to the seaside, but also to the country. Sometimes we went walking, cycling, fishing or golfing, and occasionally we took short trips to the Continent in pursuit of sun or snow. The lure of France and, later, Spain became increasingly irresistible from the 1960s, and so was born the package holiday, linked inextricably to the rise of popular air travel. This book documents our holidays and the choices we made. Coming as they do from generally anonymous family albums, the photographs have a universality that enables us all to look back at the way we were.

△ By the 1930s car ownership was more common, so more and more people chose touring holidays. For a long while, roads remained delightfully empty, making explorations of regions such as Scotland or Wales very enjoyable.

△ Railway companies were keen promoters of holiday traffic, and did much to develop the holiday habit. This wonderfully posed photograph, probably taken in a studio, was issued by the Great Western Railway to encourage holidays by train to the West Country.

△ Famous resorts such as Scarborough offered a variety of entertainments, including Pierrot shows on the beach. This card, written in 1904, shows a lively Edwardian beach scene. The message is a long story about tame rabbits escaping during a game of croquet.

△ Family albums, many of which are sadly now separated from their original owners, often contain evocative images of family holidays by the seaside. In this 1930s example the children play on the sand while the adults look on over the breakwater.

△ The specialist holiday included visits to spas, health hydros and convalescent homes. Many were set up by companies for the benefit of employees. Railway companies had many convalescent homes, including this one in Herne Bay, still in use in the 1960s.

◁ The walking holiday became increasingly popular in the 1930s. In another photograph from a family album, this girl has paused to enjoy the Derbyshire scenery.

△ Winter sports holidays, too, grew in popularity from the 1930s. These young men, neatly dressed in pullovers, ties and cravats, are enjoying themselves in Austria.

*JOHN BULL* WAS A POPULAR general interest magazine, published weekly. This cover, from the issue dated 6 September 1958, captures the excitement of the family seaside holiday.

THE CORPORATIONS and town councils of many resorts published promotional handbooks. This one is from 1961.

# Burnham-on-Sea
## Somerset
### for Leisure and Pleasure

DONKEYS, SANDCASTLES and seaside fun on the Somerset coast are the themes for the cover of the official guide issued by Burnham-on-Sea and Highbridge in 1955.

# WHERE SHALL WE GO?

FOR A HUNDRED YEARS the annual holiday has been a major event in the lives of many families. Few individual or family activities arouse such anticipation, excitement and debate – and potentially such disappointment. The success of any holiday is all in the planning, but the real difficulty is choice. In the 1920s and 1930s most people were content with a week by the seaside. They travelled by train and often stayed in the same place and in the same hotel every year. There were coach tours and early all-inclusive holidays and there were holiday camps, but the choice was limited. The spread of private car ownership brought more options, including touring, camping and caravanning. By the 1950s expanded and speedier ferry services had brought Ireland and the continent of Europe much closer, so further choices emerged. The adventurous might go cruising. A network of internal and European air services had emerged in

W. Alexander & Sons    Season 1960
## Holiday Coach Tours
from GLASGOW

BLUEBIRD

TOURS

...ur Holidays....

BRITISH RAILWAYS
# HOLIDAY GUIDE
EASTERN and NORTH EASTERN REGIONS

1/-    1949

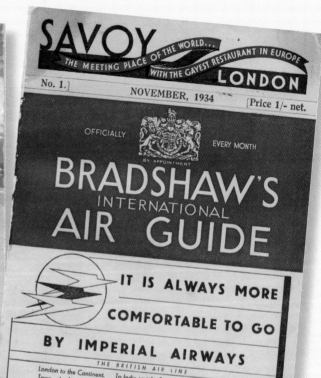

SAVOY
THE MEETING PLACE OF THE WORLD...
WITH THE GAYEST RESTAURANT IN EUROPE    LONDON

No. 1.    NOVEMBER, 1934    [Price 1/- net.

OFFICIALLY    BY APPOINTMENT    EVERY MONTH

## BRADSHAW'S
INTERNATIONAL
# AIR GUIDE

IT IS ALWAYS MORE
COMFORTABLE TO GO
BY IMPERIAL AIRWAYS
THE BRITISH AIR LINE

London to the Continent.    To India and the East.    Through Africa to Cape
Town ★ Imperial Airways Ltd., Airway Terminus, Victoria Station, London
Telephone: VICtoria 2211 (Day & Night) and the principal travel agents.
For particulars of Imperial Airways services see Tables 27, 32, 34, 36, 37, 237, 238

EASTER
1939
April 7th—10th, 1939.

ATTRACTIVE
ARRANGEMENTS
AT HOME
AND ABROAD

NELSONS TOURS LTD.
8, GRAND BUILDINGS
TRAFALGAR SQUARE
LONDON, W.C.2.

Telegrams:    Telephones:
NELTRAVEX, RAND,    WHItehall 8343
LONDON    3 lines

WHITE STAR LINE
SUNSHINE CRUISES
1932 - 1933
THE MEDITERRANEAN · SPAIN · PORTUGAL · ATLANTIC ISLES
NORTH AFRICA · RIVIERA · EGYPT & THE HOLY LAND

the late 1930s, but aircraft were still small and fares expensive. It was not until the 1960s that air travel became cheaper and more accessible, giving birth to the package-tour industry.

The planning of a holiday usually involves a mixture of fantasy and practicality. The dreams are created by advertisements; the practical information, on which success depends, is supplied by brochures, maps and guides. The first choice to be made is the type of holiday: a holiday camp, a beach holiday, a coach tour, a trip to the Continent, a flight to somewhere exotic, or a cruise? The next decision is the destination. For much of the 20th century, for most people, the choice was limited to the British Isles. For families it was usually a beach holiday, but was it to be the West Country, Wales, East Anglia or the North East Coast? And then there were walking and touring holidays in Scotland and other areas of great natural beauty. This infinite diversity complicated those choices, which is why so many families returned to the same place year after year. For everyone else, a gradual shift from fantasy to reality eventually led to a decision, and the holiday was booked.

## ALL-IN HOLIDAY IN SCOTLAND

### FROM
### £14-19-0

CHILDREN UNDER 14) £10-12-6
ACCOMPANYING ADULTS

*inclusive of*

TRAVEL TICKETS : GUARANTEED SEAT ON TRAINS :
ACCOMMODATION : SIGHTSEEING TRIPS : MEALS ON
TRAINS : GRATUITIES

*from*

SHEFFIELD, ROTHERHAM, DONCASTER,
LEEDS, BRADFORD, HUDDERSFIELD,
HALIFAX, KEIGHLEY, HARROGATE,
SCARBOROUGH, HULL and neighbouring
towns

EACH SATURDAY from JUNE 7th to SEPTEMBER 6th 1952
returning the following Saturday
(Longer periods can be arranged)

### A WEEK — OR MORE
### IN BONNIE SCOTLAND !

Arranged by the Creative Tourist Agents' Conference in conjunction
with British Railways

For further information and booking form with conditions of issue, apply to British
Railways Stations, Offices, and the usual rail ticket agencies

*aledonia.*

### HIC STUDIES OF
### N COE

## SCARBOROUGH
### THE TONIC HOLIDAY

### THE HOLIDAY FOR YOU
### GLORIOUS SANDS — TONIC AIR — ENDLESS ENTERTAINMENT

You are bound to have a lovely time at Scarborough. For this, the queen of northern
pleasure resorts, offers everything you expect from a holiday. There are miles of superb
sands, the sea is safe, the air is tonic and the surroundings beautiful. There is every popular
sport and entertainment for every age.

The gay, colourful Spa, Ballrooms, Concert Parties, Cinemas and the unique Open-Air Theatre,
provide endless entertainment, and there are two magnificent open-air swimming pools.

Here is a seaside resort of lovely flower-bedecked gardens and spacious parks set in
country of great historical interest. It is a TONIC HOLIDAY — it is Scarborough
— it is the holiday for YOU. Write for full particulars to the Visitors' Service Bureau,
(Dept. G.1), Town Hall, Scarborough.

| SHELL | THE SHILLING GUIDES | BP |

### DEVON

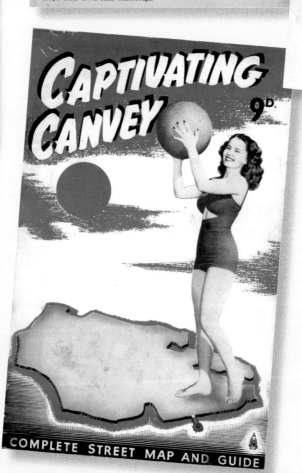

## Captivating
## Canvey
9D.

### COMPLETE STREET MAP AND GUIDE

## ABERYSTWYTH

VISION OF ENGLAND, General editors Clough and

### NORTHUMBERLAND

TYPICALLY STYLISH, this poster was published by PLM (the Paris, Lyon, Méditerranée railway), to promote the attractions of Vichy, in France, in 1929. The artist was Roger Broders.

BRITISH RAILWAYS in 1956 was heavily involved in tourism, tempting holidaymakers with rail, bus and steamer tours.

ANOTHER RAILWAY POSTER, designed for the London & North Eastern Railway in 1935 by Frank Newbold, promoted Harwich as the gateway to Belgium and the Netherlands.

# POSTCARDS

THE SENDING OF POSTCARDS is one of the great holiday rituals. It all started in the early 1900s, when the General Post Office allowed picture cards to be posted without an envelope. Initially, there was no room for a message on the back, but soon the standard card, with divided back, appeared, causing an immediate sensation. There were many types: topographic, artistic, humorous, vulgar, colour-printed and photographic. Photographs could also be printed on to blank postcards, creating potentially unique images.

On the Sands                    Brighton.

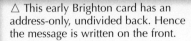

GREETINGS FROM DEDHAM

The sea-weed smells very strong down here.

△ This early Brighton card has an address-only, undivided back. Hence the message is written on the front.

◁ Artist-drawn vulgar and double-entendre cards appeared early, often printed in Germany for the UK.

▽ Busy beach scenes based on photographs were popular, in colour and monochrome. This is at Rhyl.

△ The multiview card has always been a favourite. This one was posted in Colchester in 1917 by a soldier writing to tell a friend when his leave would start.

▷ This is an example of a novelty card with a fold-out of local views. Such cards were available in many resorts around Britain.

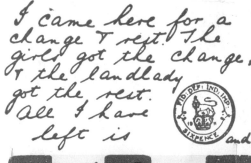

I came here for a change & rest. The girls got the change, & the landlady got the rest. All I have left is

Sands looking East, Rhyl.

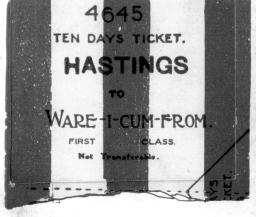

4645
TEN DAYS TICKET.
HASTINGS
TO
WARE-I-CUM-FROM.
FIRST      CLASS.
Not Transferable.

GODSHILL CHURCH.
ISLE OF WIGHT.

MR & MRS. S. GULL, PENZANCE.

△ Postcard puns are very common. This 1950s example from Penzance features Mr & Mrs S Gull.

◁ Many cards reproduced paintings and watercolour sketches by well-known artists, often in series. This Isle of Wight scene was posted in 1906.

▽ A long-term favourite for the lazy holidaymaker is the tick-box card. This version was issued in the 1950s by the Butlin's holiday camp at Margate.

▷ The classic artist-drawn, humorous seaside postcard emerged in the Edwardian era and has remained an integral part of seaside holidays ever since.

▽ Another pun card, this time from the 1930s and featuring Blackpool bathing belles.

'Fraid it's a bit nippy down here

174

Too busy to write - sending this
*Lazy-gram*
from MARGATE

| HI THERE : | I AM : | I WISH YOU WOULD: | THIS PLACE IS : |
|---|---|---|---|
| Toots | Fine | Write | Worth Seeing |
| Mamma | Sober | Send more money | Wonderful |
| Papa | Happy | Come here | Terrific |
| Office Pals | In a Dream | Love me | Not so hot |
| Sweetheart | Still Single | Send me your photo | Tempting |
| Folks | Courting | Wait for me | Dry |
| Brother | | | Exciting |
| Sister | THE WEATHER IS : | | |
| | Grand | | I'M DOING LOTS OF : |
| I NEED : | Lousy | YOURS : | Dancing |
| You | Perfect | With love | Sun Bathing |
| Loving | Very Dry | Forever | Swimming |
| Cash | Darned Hot | Sincerely | Drinking |
| More Cash | Pouring | | Fishing ? |
| Kisses | | | Shows |
| Mothering | I MISS | | Fiddling |
| Smothering | You | I WILL BE SEEING YOU : | Sight-seeing |
| Rest | The folks | Soon | Making Whoopee |
| Sympathy | Home | Someday | Thinking of you |
| Aspirins | The Office (Don't think) | Maybe | Sssh ! |

(Tick off items wanted X)

From    Date

Registered copyright

JUST A FEW LINES

C667

# HOLIDAY SNAPS

THE FIRST TRULY AMATEUR and easily portable, roll-film camera was the famous Box Brownie, launched by Kodak in 1900. From this point, generations of relatively foolproof cameras made the family photograph commonplace. Initially, camera and film had to be returned to the maker for processing, printing and reloading, but soon chemists and photography shops were offering these services and decorative paper wallets for negatives and prints came into being. Endlessly varied, all are richly reflective of their period.

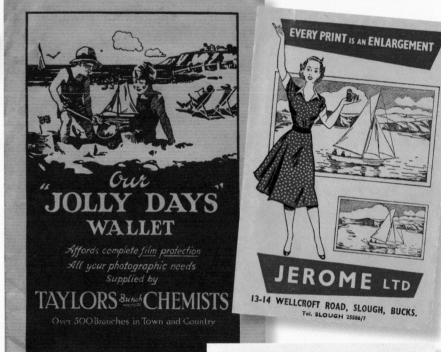

△▷ Kodak was the great name associated with the amateur camera. A famous icon on Kodak film wallets was a girl in a striped dress. Emerging in the early 1900s, she was used through the 1920s and 1930s, her dress being altered to suit changing fashion. She was a consistent element, while others, such as that on the Timothy Whites & Taylors example, were more eccentric and short-lived.

△ Equally familiar were the names of national chains of chemists' shops that offered photographic services. They also issued wallets with characterful images printed on them. Typical is this Taylors example with its evocative 1920s beach scene. Jerome, by contrast, used their version of the Kodak girl over a considerable period, usually superimposed on images of photographs. Throughout this period, wallets had drawn, rather than photographic, illustrations.

▷ Frith's, a smaller chain, for a while used this very distinctive image. For their sporty girl, they reduced the Kodak striped dress to a bikini, and accompanied her with a strange, penguin-like creature made from pieces of film.

"Hold on, lady, IT'LL NEED TWO PLATES TO TAKE YOU!"

Today's leader in photog...

**ILFORD** naturally...

ILFORD FILMS

BROWNIE
STARMITE
Camera

BATTERY - CAPACITOR MODEL

△◁ Prior to the amateur camera, photography was a cumbersome business, with bulky equipment and long exposure times. Many people relied on the travelling photographer to take pictures for them, as these cards indicate.

◁ The Brownie camera went through many refinements. This brochure is for a 1950s model which, despite flash attachment and modern styling, was still foolproof.

▽ For the many who did not own a camera, photographic prints of local views were widely available, individually and in sets. This Isle of Wight pack is from the 1930s.

12 BEAUTIFUL PHOTO SNAPSHOTS OF LOCAL VIEWS

PRICE 1/-

Published by W. J. NIGH & SONS, VENTNOR, I.W.    Copyright Photographs.

ILFORD FILMS

◁△ Another big name is Ilford, and their wallets from the 1950s and 1960s were stylish and memorable, featuring both drawn and photographic images. It is interesting that some of these girls are wearing stripes.

# STUDIO PORTRAITS

THE DEVELOPMENT OF PHOTOGRAPHY from its invention in the 1830s was remarkably rapid, and by the 1850s people from all walks of life were having their images recorded by studio photographers. The most familiar form was the small *carte de visite* portrait photograph, but many larger formats were also available. At this point, glass negatives were used, from which paper prints were made and mounted on cards, often with the photographer's name. Not much changed until the amateur, portable camera emerged in the early 1900s. However, the studio photographer lived on and people continued to visit for formal or group portraits. Studios, notably those at holiday resorts, were equipped with painted backdrops and unusual props, which add interest to the portrait.

△ A wonderful 1930s group poses in a Blackpool studio, complete with old motorbike, stuffed pony and large toy dog.

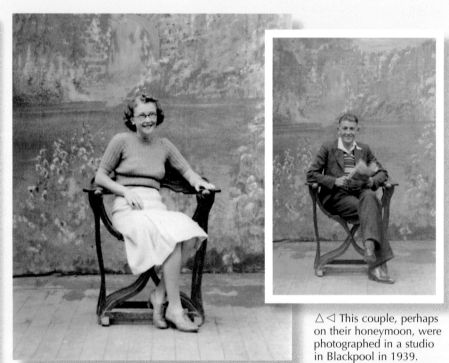

△ ◁ This couple, perhaps on their honeymoon, were photographed in a studio in Blackpool in 1939.

△ The painted backdrop reveals that this couple are in a studio, and their old car is a photographer's prop.

△ '… a painted ship upon a painted ocean.'

△ Some photographers' props were truly extraordinary. These two small boys, clutching their wooden seaside spades, were photographed in Portobello, Scotland, in July 1916, balanced on a stuffed donkey.

△ Crudely painted boats form a backdrop to this elegant girl from Treherbert. She sent the photograph to 'Dear Bert' in August 1915, 'in loving remembrance of happy times spent together'.

△ An Edwardian child poses in a studio in Hastings on a make-believe beach decorated with real rocks and imitation seaweed.

△ Wilfred Ernest Kingston on his third birthday, 1st June 1909.

△ This small *carte de visite* photograph, taken in Penzance in about 1870, shows George Harpur Bazeley in his holiday clothes. The real rope adds a seaside flavour.

# SOUVENIRS

HOLIDAYS ARE ABOUT MEMORIES, and souvenirs are the things we take home to prompt those memories. The development of the souvenir trade was, therefore, linked closely to the growth of resorts and the holiday business generally. From an early date, certain souvenirs were, and still are, associated with particular places, for example marquetry woodware from Tunbridge Wells, sand paintings from the Isle of Wight or Blue John from Derbyshire, but by the late-Victorian era souvenirs of a less specific nature, such as seashell ornaments, were widely available. The souvenir or gift shop became an integral feature of every tourist town and region, selling a huge range of cheaply produced merchandise, much of which was made far from the resort in which it was being sold.

◁▽ For many, the simplest and most easily accessible souvenir was the picture postcard. In the Edwardian era, these became increasingly elaborate and decorative, with many clearly made to be kept rather than posted. Choosing cards from the rotating displays became an important holiday ritual.

▷ Souvenir and gift shops had to carry huge stocks of wares aimed at the popular market, along with more exclusive and locally produced lines. In many areas, the holiday trade was seasonal, so the shopkeepers had to make the most of it. The Drug Stores at Gronant seemed to sell everything, while the little Ladyefayre shop in Devon concentrated on local products. Pottery was always popular, especially the vast selection of badged souvenir porcelain miniatures that were made in Staffordshire by Goss and other companies from the late-Victorian period onwards.

GRN. 601.

Model of Ancient
British
Bronze Pot.
618

BIDEFORD

TRENT

OPEN ALL DAY
EA TROOPS RECREATION

Ladyefayre

BRASSWARE

DEVONWARE

ORES CNT.

Kodak Film

Developing and Printing

QUICK SERVICE

DRUG STORES. GRONANT.

## LOCAL SOUVENIRS

Arbroath smokies
Bakewell tart
Blackpool rock
Brighton rock
Bristol glass
Cornish cream, fudge, pasties, serpentine
Cromer crab
Derbyshire Blue John
Devon pottery, motto ware, fudge
Dorset fudge
Dundee marmalade
Edinburgh rock
Eccles cakes
Guernsey jumpers
Harrogate toffee
Honiton lace
Irish bog-oak carvings
Isle of Harris tweed
Isle of Wight coloured sands
Kendal mint cake
Luton straw hats
Lyme Regis fossils
Melton Mowbray pies
Model London buses, telephone kiosks
Pontefract cakes
Poole pottery
Scottish agate, malt whisky, shortbread, tartan
Shetland knitwear
Tunbridge ware
Welsh love spoons, weaving
Whitby jet
Worcester porcelain

# OUR WEEK IN CORNWALL – AUGUST 1936

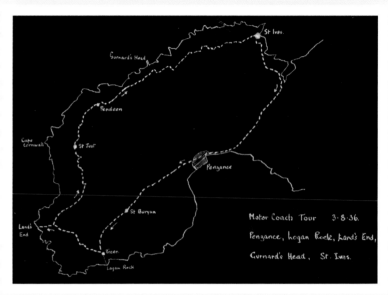

1. We all took the 10.30 from Paddington, the Cornish Riviera Express.

2. The view from our Penzance hotel, the Polytechnic, looking towards Newlyn.

3. The route of the motor coach tour on 3rd August: Penzance, Logan Rock, Land's End, Gurnard's Head, St Ives.

4. Here we all are at Land's End, on the very tip of England.

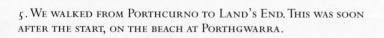

5. We walked from Porthcurno to Land's End. This was soon after the start, on the beach at Porthgwarra.

6. A welcome bit of rest after lunch.

7. A view of the magnificent offshore rocks, Enys Dodnan and Armed Knight, near Land's End. Longships lighthouse in the distance.

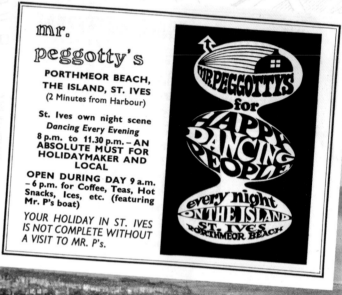

# ST IVES

GLORIOUS BEACHES and a magnificent setting turned this little Cornish fishing village into a major resort in the late-Victorian era. Also important was its discovery by the landscape and genre painters of the Newlyn School, the first wave of artists who put St Ives firmly on the map. Others followed, notably in the 1930s and the 1950s, giving the region a particular appeal and an international reputation among generations of visitors.

**mr. peggotty's**

PORTHMEOR BEACH,
THE ISLAND, ST. IVES
(2 Minutes from Harbour)

St. Ives own night scene
*Dancing Every Evening*
8 p.m. to 11.30 p.m. – AN
ABSOLUTE MUST FOR
HOLIDAYMAKER AND
LOCAL

OPEN DURING DAY 9 a.m.
– 6 p.m. for Coffee, Teas, Hot
Snacks, Ices, etc. (featuring
Mr. P's boat)

YOUR HOLIDAY IN ST. IVES
IS NOT COMPLETE WITHOUT
A VISIT TO MR. P's.

MR.PEGGOTTYS for HAPPY DANCING PEOPLE
every night
ON THE ISLAND
ST. IVES
PORTHMEOR BEACH

ST. IVES CORNWALL.

▲ This 1969 guidebook, issued by the Borough of St Ives, reflects both artistic traditions and fine beaches.

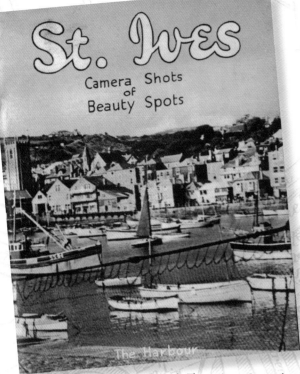

St. Ives

Camera Shots
of
Beauty Spots

The Harbour

THE HARBOUR. ST. IVES. 6052

▼ This 1906 view shows Porthminster beach, the station and the harbour.

▲ The painter Samuel John Lamorna Birch wrote the introduction to this 1930s photo guide.

THE COUNCIL'S OFFICIAL GUIDE

THE
HOMELAND 7d. Net.
7d. Net. HANDBOOKS

St. IVES
(Cornwall)

WITH ITS SURROUNDINGS
ORDNANCE MAP

St. Ives: Of all Booksellers, Bookstalls and Newsagents.

THE HOMELAND ASSOCIATION, Ltd.,
37 & 38 MAIDEN LANE,
COVENT GARDEN, LONDON, W.C.2.

VOL. 78 OF THE SERIES

EIGHTH EDITION

▲ This guide is from a 1920s series.

G.W.R.

St. Ives

▲ This view of St Ives harbour dates from the 1950s.

◄ The Great Western Railway arrived in 1877.

▼ A 1930s artistic postcard view of an artistic town.

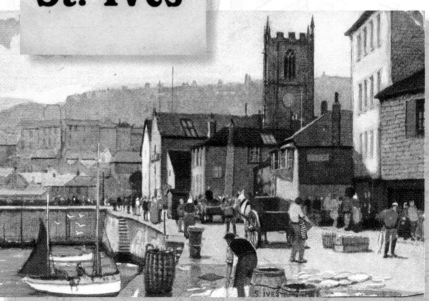

# WHERE WE STAYED

" *The great advantage of a hotel is that it's a refuge from home life.* "

GEORGE BERNARD SHAW (1856–1950)

# HOTELS

HOLIDAY RESORTS AND HOTELS developed side by side, mainly in the late 1800s. The railway network actively encouraged the spread of hotels, many of which were built by the railway companies themselves to bring traffic to new holiday regions. Competition ensured an interesting diversity of architectural styles and interior decor, but most important was the setting, along with the range of services and facilities offered.

Tudor Close, Ro[...]

Knoll House
Studland Bay
Dorset

Telephone-Studland 251-2
Resident Proprietors -
Col. & Mrs. Kenneth Ferguson

23573 Felixstowe. Felix Hotel.

◁ The Felix Hotel in Felixstowe, a grand late-Victorian structure, was a typical railway hotel, built by the Great Eastern to encourage the development of the village of Felixstowe into a smart seaside resort.

△ Knoll House, Studland, Dorset, laid on all kinds of activities for families. In the 1960s, challenged by the Continental holiday market, hotels in Britain had to offer more and more to stay in business.

*Hotel Monico*

THE PROMENADE, CANVEY

FULLY LICENSED ATTRACTIVE BARS

H. & C. in all Bedrooms

Fitted Slumber Mattresses.

CENTRAL HEATING THROUGHOUT

:: **SPECIAL WINTER TERMS** ::

Phone : Canvey 26

BEACH HOTEL ◆ GOREY ◆ JERSEY

△ Small hotels in minor resorts had to work hard to attract customers and many, such as the Hotel Monico in Canvey Island, relied on their name.

▷ To us the Beach Hotel in Gorey, Jersey, looks decidedly staid, but this typical 1970s publicity postcard would have appealed in its day.

Derwentwater Hotel. Portinscale.

Abraham's Series No. 419. Keswick.

◁ The claims of the Tudor Close Hotel, near Brighton, to be 'the Loveliest Hotel on the South Coast' seem a bit outrageous, but they may well have succeeded in bringing in the clients.

△ This 1907 card shows a smart hotel in the Lake District, but the message on the back reveals that the writer was actually staying in a boarding house in Keswick.

▽ With many hotels refusing to take children at all, the Kimberley, in Westgate-on-Sea, Kent, made a point of trying to attract young families.

...n, Brighton, the Loveliest Hotel on the South Coast.

"Eh, Miss, dost tha' have babies in this hotel?"
"Not personally, Madam!"

KIMBERLEY HOTEL, WESTGATE-ON-SEA, KENT.     "FOR PEOPLE WITH CHILDREN ONLY"

▷ Llandrindod Wells was a famous spa town in the Edwardian era, when this card was posted. It offered a range of grand hotels for those coming to take the waters or simply seeking a healthy holiday in the heart of Wales.

▽ The Grange Hotel in Harrogate issued this smart brochure in the 1930s. The garden, it says, was 'a veritable sun trap', and full board cost from 7 guineas (£7.35) per week.

△ This 1930s brochure for the Sundrum Castle claims it to be 'Ayrshire's foremost hotel', making much of its location in Burns country as well as its facilities for riding, golf and fishing.

▷ The Furness Abbey was another railway hotel, run by the small but very ambitious Furness Railway, the company largely responsible for the development of Cumbria as a holiday region.

▷ This 1911 card shows Minehead's Hotel Metropole at its best, surrounded by extensive grounds and offering excellent views across the bay.

▷ ▽ In the Edwardian period and the 1920s, conservatories and sun rooms were popular in hotels. Characteristically there was a hint of the exotic in their decor, with details such as palms, wicker furniture and eastern carpets – all seen here in the Palm Court at the Royal Exeter Hotel, Bournemouth. The Conservatory at the Deanston House Hotel, in Doune, was a rather grander affair, with white tablecloths and waitresses in starched aprons.

THE NEW PALM COURT. ROYAL EXETER HOTEL. BOURNEMOUTH.

## HOTEL LUNCHEONS

For many holidaymakers, a stay in an hotel meant only one thing, and that was full board, with all meals included in the price. Despite the holiday or resort setting, the hotel luncheon was often quite a grand affair, with full waiter service and none of the self-service buffets so common in recent times. Children would have to return from the beach in order to change for lunch and, after ploughing through several courses in a rather grown-up environment, would probably have to have a rest before they could get on with their holiday.

CONSERVATORY, DEANSTON HOUSE HOTEL, DOUNE

# BOARDING HOUSES

THE SEASIDE BOARDING HOUSE, and its landlady, have a particular place in British cultural history. It was in the late 1800s, when the paid holiday became an established tradition for the middle and working classes, that the boarding house came into its own. Soon these former domestic houses were lining the lesser streets of seaside resorts shoulder to shoulder, offering bed and breakfast or full board at fiercely competitive rates.

◁ No doubt many boarding establishments issued cards or leaflets, but few survive. This 1930s example, from The Sydney in Blackpool, seems typical. Inside, we see a week's full board cost £2 2s 0d (£2.10), with children charged according to age. There were four meals a day: breakfast, midday dinner, tea and supper.

THE SYDNEY

Boarding Establishment.

116, ALBERT ROAD, BLACKPOOL.

Prop: Mrs. J. MULLINEUX.   PHONE 1355.

▽ △ A curious phenomenon of the Edwardian era, and one that lived on into the 1920s, was the boarding house photograph. It seems that local photographers regularly visited boarding houses to capture that week's lodgers on film. The legacy of this is thousands of pictures of usually cheerful groups arranged in front of the boarding house, generally offering no clue as to date, location or identity of the randomly assembled group. These two groups, datable to the Edwardian period by the clothes, reveal predictably varied ages and dress styles.

PUBLIC & PRIVATE APARTMENTS WITH OR WITHOUT BOARD

CORDON

"They say it's impossible for three to sleep four in a bed- but we do it here and are happy!"

▷▽ Two more boarding house group photographs: the one shown left is of a comparatively small, relaxed group, taken somewhere on the Somerset coast in August 1914. Soon these cheerful young men would be in the army and going off to war. The picture below dates from the 1930s. The dress is more informal, with most of the men sporting open-necked shirts rather than ties, the children dressed comfortably and the younger women, at least, wearing their hair in contemporary styles.

△ Promotional handbooks issued annually by the town councils of many resorts used to have page after page of boarding house listings. These superior establishments are advertised in a 1950s Skegness brochure. The names are endearing, and revealing.

# CAMPING

THE PRACTICE OF CAMPING spread into the holiday from army and school life. In the early 1900s many manufacturers turned to producing lightweight and increasingly sophisticated versions of military tents and equipment for the holiday market, and by the 1920s camping had become a common family experience. This was a holiday that was economical, healthy and free from the constraints of many hotels and boarding houses.

△ A large tent has been pitched on a private campsite in a field in Sussex in 1931. A raincoat was always an essential item of clothing.

◁ This classic camping group, somewhere by the sea in the 1950s, shows happy children, complete with printed tin buckets, and mothers prepared to make the best of it.

◁ A typical family camping holiday in 1930s Britain: mum, bent double, does the washing up; dad, sitting comfortably, fiddles with some piece of equipment; their son, in his school gabardine mac, fools around with the mallet.

△ Catalogues were a key source for items of camping equipment. This one was issued by Yeo Bros. Paull & Co. of Bristol in 1938.

△ A shave in the sun was always a good start to the day, following the early morning cup of tea.

△ A page from the 1938 Yeo Paull catalogue, showing the price of tents. No.1 cost 37s 6d (£1.88).

◁ Camping was a serious business in the Edwardian era. These young men have come with a table, a chair, a tin trunk, some wooden boxes, heavy pottery mugs and an enamel jug, as well as their tent.

◁ These jolly lads were photographed in 1938. The message on the back, from Pat to his mother, says: 'Don't ask me what this card is about.'

▷ This group of young men, on a camping holiday on the Dorset coast, features on a pre-1914 card entitled 'Bachelor's Paradise'.

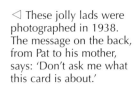

# CAMPING COACHES

IN THE MID-1930S the London, Midland & Scottish Railway (LMS), one of the four major railway companies, began to offer holidays in converted elderly railway carriages parked on quiet sidings in generally picturesque spots. Others followed, spreading a network of camping coaches all over Britain. Most were on the coast, but they were also found in remoter areas of the Lake District and Scotland. Typical coaches slept six or eight, with limited facilities: oil lighting, no running water, a key to the station lavatories. They were at their most popular in the 1950s, with 150 available on a weekly basis each season. By the late 1960s all had gone.

◁ The LMS Railway issued a series of cards to promote the new 'holiday caravans', as camping coaches were first called. This one, posted in 1940, shows an elegant and well-dressed group listening to the gramophone as they wait for dinner to be ready.

▽ The Southern Railway claimed its new 'luxury camps' had 'everything a camper would require'. A particular feature was the radio set, or wireless, seen here in a promotional photograph from 1936.

△ This London & North Eastern Railway (LNER) publicity picture shows the limited catering facilities, including a paraffin stove, in one of its camping coaches.

◁ Another LMS promotional postcard, sent in 1937, shows a group of happy campers arriving at their remotely sited holiday caravan.

▷ British Railways carried on the camping-coach network after nationalization. In the 1950s, when this brochure was issued, a camping coach cost between £5 and £12 per week, depending on size and season.

An LMS Holiday Caravan

▽ This delightful view of washing day at a camping coach in a peaceful siding somewhere in Essex was issued as a promotional photograph by the LNER in 1935.

BRITISH RAILWAYS.

# CAMPING COACHES
## for delightful inexpensive holidays
## 1957

LIVING ROOM
EASTERN REGION
CAMPING COACH

### Camping Coaches provide

- Holidays in specially selected places in England, Scotland and Wales
- Out of doors camping holiday with the comfort of well-appointed living accommodation at reasonable cost
- A cheap and ideal holiday for the family

Apply to the addresses shown under "Location of Coaches and Rental Charges"

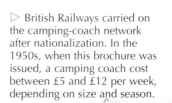

A WESTERN REGION CAMPING COACH

# CARAVANNING

THE EARLIEST HOLIDAY CARAVANS were adapted from horse-drawn gypsy vans and military, agricultural or commercial road vehicles. The production of caravans specifically designed to be towed by private cars began in the 1920s and was well established by the 1930s, with styles either traditional or consciously modern. The 1950s witnessed a vast expansion in the industry, as caravanning became increasingly popular.

◁▽ Caravan parks began to proliferate along Britain's coastline in the 1930s, initially without any planning controls. The random and often incredibly crowded nature of many early parks can be seen below at Sea View Camp, Preston, near Weymouth, in the 1960s. However, planning laws soon brought order out of chaos, along with support facilities such as sanitation and camp shops (left).

△ The earliest factory-built caravans were often quite small, reflecting the low power of the average family car of that era and the limited amount of equipment considered necessary. As can be seen, many dog-owners leapt at the possibility that caravanning gave them of taking their pets on holiday – something that was not often possible with other types of accommodation.

43279    SEA VIEW CAMP, PRESTON, WEYMOUTH.

△ The pleasures of caravanning were widely enjoyed. Here, in 1951, a couple have parked their two-tone Wolseley and the typically small caravan of the era in a pleasant grassy field, far from the crowds.

△ One of the best-known caravan names was Bluebird, a group incorporating a number of manufacturers. This 1960s brochure promotes the Wren Continental: 'a colourful, bright and chirpy little caravan ... everything you can desire for fast touring or lazy weekends. Its modest dimensions retain a compelling air of spaciousness. Homely comfort and faraway places whenever you want.' The price was £269.

▽ In the early days caravans were often converted from other road vehicles. Some time in the 1930s, an old bus enjoys retirement as a spacious caravan, with a coat of fresh paint and pretty curtains at the windows.

GREETINGS *from* CARA-CARS LTD. ILKLEY

WHARFEDALE RAILWAY

*Caravanning without petrol.*

DRIVER G. KILBURN            GUARD B. HUTCHINGS

△ This bizarre image from the heart of Yorkshire suggests how to carry on caravanning during wartime petrol restrictions: make use of the local miniature railway!

▽ A 1930s family poses outside this rather basic caravan. At that time the vans were largely for sleeping, and domestic activities such as eating took place outdoors, weather permitting.

△ Early caravanning photographs are always intriguing, often revealing unusual and home-made vehicles with eccentric features, such as bow windows. This distinctive late-1920s or early-1930s caravan could have started life as a commercial road vehicle. Camping and caravanning went together in those days and, as seen here, a tent was often pitched beside the caravan to deal with any overcrowding.

△▽▷ In 1923 the Bowkers, from Hampshire, went on a caravan holiday with some friends. They used two vehicles, both of which were probably converted from commercial road vans. They were towed by their one horse, so progress would have been slow. Most of the party took bicycles, and no doubt went ahead to find suitable camping grounds and stock up on provisions.

Above: hitched up and ready for the off. Below: after a long day on the road, tea was something to look forward to. The bicycles are parked and someone has washed the clothes. Centre right: the folding furniture and the amount of crockery and cooking utensils suggest the vans were very well equipped. Top right: the inside of this caravan was beautifully but traditionally fitted, and the bunks had plenty of light from the various windows. Far right: there are always chores to be done: this girl is clearly not enjoying her turn at washing up.

# CHALET BUNGALOWS

THE SEASIDE CHALET is the most extreme example of the Englishman's home being his castle. Initially these wooden structures were often home-made and generally quite whimsical, but gradually some standard features appeared, including verandahs, casement windows and a range of decorative details such as bargeboarding. In the early 1900s, chalets were offered for sale in kit form – simple versions for day use and larger, more sophisticated ones designed to accommodate a family on holiday. Never conceived for permanent use, they were nonetheless increasingly built in groups around shared facilities such as washrooms and shops.

▽ This grand chalet was built in 1912 by the Dorset family assembled here, along with the cat, soon after its completion. Although it is a holiday home and the facilities are basic, everyone is looking remarkably smart – even the children.

▷ By the 1920s chalets were appearing in rows, and even whole estates. Two typical factory-built types can be seen here: the verandah style, and a simpler version with Art Deco sunburst decoration over the door.

▷ This girl and her dog enjoy the sunshine on the steps of their chalet. Inside there is ample room for the table, laid for tea, complete with cloth and vase of flowers.

▽ The eccentricity and diversity of the chalet knows no bounds and is always part of the appeal. These Edwardian ladies and gentlemen have a superb example, with rustic wooden screen, hanging baskets and even a cannon. Truly, an Englishman's home is his castle!

△ It is also teatime for this 1930s family, gathered round the table outside a substantial and permanent-looking chalet and all wearing splendidly period clothing.

**SEASCAPE BUNGALETS** EYPE

◁ Estates of identical chalets, designed to be hired by holidaymakers by the week, spread rapidly around Britain's coastline. This is an early 1960s Dorset version, promoted under an exciting new name worthy of John Betjeman!

## CREAM TEAS

*Apparently the Devon cream tea started in a Benedictine abbey in Tavistock. Having been plundered and badly damaged by the Vikings in 997AD, it was restored by Ordulf, Earl of Devon, whose father had built the original abbey. Ordulf was so pleased by the help offered by local people that he asked the monks to reward them with large portions of bread spread with jam and cream. This proved so popular that the monks continued to serve visitors and travellers with similar fare – and so the Devon cream tea was born.*

▽ It is the 1920s and this family is very proud of its new car and its new chalet, a substantial structure clearly capable of comfortably housing the five children plus various friends and relatives.

# CLARACH BAY
## CHALET & CARAVAN PARK
### Near ABERYSTWYTH

Situated in the most picturesque valley of this beautiful Welsh Mountain Scenery. Every Chalet has a delightful view of both the Bay, the Sea and the rolling Hills surrounding the Valley.

Our Chalet Park is the ideal centre for touring the whole of Mid-Wales.

## Super Comfort De Luxe Chalets

EVERY CHALET ACCOMMO-DATES SIX PERSONS

EVERY CHALET HAS ITS OWN FLUSH TOILET.

EVERY CHALET HAS MAINS RUNNING WATER IN KITCHENETTE.

EVERY CHALET HAS ELEC-TRICITY FOR COOK-ING, LIGHTING, HEATING.

EVERY CHALET HAS TWO SEPARATE BED-ROOMS, LOUNGE, KITCHENETTE.

EVERY CHALET HAS COM-FORTABLE SPRING INTERIOR BEDS.

View of Lounge with Bedrooms opening off

### TERMS

s. 0d. — £16 16s. 0d. per week.

cial reduced rates for Early

d Late Season bookings.

ND FOR BROCHURE
to
oliday Chalets
per King Street
LEICESTER

View of Children's Bedrooms

◁ By the 1950s chalet parks were common in many parts of Britain. At this stage, before the development of the semi-permanent mobile home, parks often offered a choice of caravans or chalets. The leaflet for this park in Wales shows off its best features: the view and, in the chalets, the kitchenette, the flush toilet and the comfortable beds. Prices ranged from £6 6s 0d to £16 16s 0d (£6.30 to £16.80) per week.

▽ The chalet park required support facilities such as the shop. This picture gives an insight into the favoured chalet holiday diet of the early 1960s – plenty of tinned food and fish fingers!

# HOLIDAY CAMPS

So-called holiday camps existed in a very basic form from the early 1900s, but the revolution came in 1936, when Billy Butlin opened his first camp at Skegness, setting new standards for high-quality, all-inclusive, low-cost family holidays. Other Butlin's camps followed, along with many set up by imitators, and by the 1950s the holiday camp was well rooted at the heart of British culture, where it survives to this day.

▽ This is the 1946 brochure for the Brean Sands Holiday Resort in Somerset, selling the classic holiday camp experience: 'All days are glorious at Brean Sands', 'The ruling spirit of the Camp is individual freedom', 'Meals are important', 'Please bring your ration book'. Inclusive terms for a week were 5 guineas (£5.25) per person.

▷ Typical of the minor camps that rivalled Butlin's, Dene's was near Lowestoft, in Suffolk. This card, sent in 1956, says it all: 'Having a lovely time. Lots to do, plenty to eat.'

▷ Holiday camp publicity is often revealing. The 1950s Minster Beach example managed to make the Isle of Sheppey seem appealing, while the 1949 Middleton Tower leaflet took the theme of a cruise on land, with echoes of a famous Cunard liner.

▽ It's teatime at Pakefield Hall, a Suffolk holiday camp opened in the 1930s, and the tables, set with large teapots, are full.

SMILING SOMERSET

BREAN SANDS HOLIDAY RESORT

SECTION OF DINING HALL, P

## Right by the Sea!

### MINSTER BEACH HOLIDAY CAMP

not a big Camp but its friendly atmosphere ensures a

### HAPPY HOLIDAY FOR **ALL** THE FAMILY

Ward's Hill, Minster-on-Sea,
Isle of Sheppey, Kent

▷ The first holiday camps were very basic, temporary and probably inspired by army camps. Nevertheless, these Edwardian lads seem to be having a good time in their tent at Lucas's camp, near Blackpool.

HOLIDAY CAMP NORBRECK BLACKPOOL.

LANCASHIRE COAST & WIRRAL PENINSULA (CHESHIRE)
★ ★ ★ ★ ★ THE NEW ★ ★ ★ ★ ★
### S.S. BERENGARIA
the "CRUISING ON LAND" Holiday
as it will appear when ready for launching in May 1949.

### MIDDLETON TOWER
BRITAIN'S BEST
### HOLIDAY CAMP
will be open for 1949 Season

AMENITIES GREATER THAN EVER
THE PERFECT FAMILY
HOLIDAY · SOMETHING FOR EVERYONE!
AT A COST TO SUIT EVERY PURSE

OPENS MAY 14th, 1949
Send for illustrated Brochure    Middleton Tower Holiday Camp near Morecambe

PRESTATYN HOLIDAY CAMP, THE SWIM POOL

85657

HALL HOLIDAY CAMP

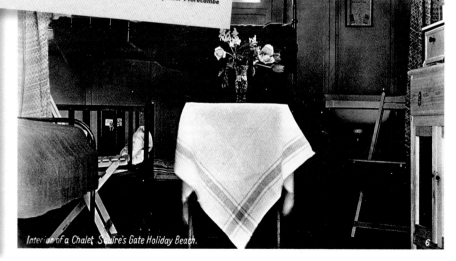

Interior of a Chalet Squire's Gate Holiday Beach.

6

△ Maritime echoes were popular at holiday camps. This is Prestatyn, in north Wales, in 1947, showing an interesting range of holiday fashions. Ken writes: 'Marvellous bar, real good strong beer.'

◁ This card shows us inside a chalet at an early camp. The beds, furniture and fittings are basic, but there is a washbasin. The cloth and flowers were probably put on the table just for the photograph. The only picture is a Wills cigarette advertisement.

▷ These happy campers have just arrived at Butlin's, in August 1949, and have been caught by the camp's photographer. They would soon be given their hand-made enamel badges, which they would wear throughout their stay and keep with pride after the holiday was over.

▽ By the 1950s Butlin's had six camps, in England, Scotland, Wales and Ireland (and three more were to open in the 1960s). Their stylish advertising made the most of this 'coast to coast' coverage, tempting their loyal clientele to visit other sites.

Greetings from PONTIN'S
MIDDLETON TOWER HOLIDAY CAMP

△ The 1960s and 1970s were difficult times for British holiday camps but many managed to keep going despite the challenge of the Continental package. This is a typical postcard of that period, from a well-known Lancashire camp.

▽ Bognor Regis has long been a famous name in Butlin's history. Captured here is that magic moment when the 'Redcoat' in charge of the camp radio plays the chimes before making an announcement. This postcard was sent in 1963 by Lesley to her aunt, to say she was having a wonderful time and the food and the chalet were lovely.

SPEND YOUR *Holiday* AT

*Butlin's*

GLASGOW

BEAUTIFUL
HOLIDAY
VILLAGE

**AYR**

SCOTLAND

Send now for full particulars, illustrated brochure and booking form to—

**BUTLIN'S Ltd.**
(Dept. HB) 439 Oxford St., LONDON, W.1.

or apply to principal travel agencies.

THERE is no more perfect setting for a holiday than the West Coast of Scotland—and no spot so ideal as the Heads of Ayr where Butlin's Holiday Village offers you all that is best in holiday values. Make up your mind NOW that you'll have the best time of your life in 1949 — at Butlin's Holiday Village, Ayr.
The Tariffs are inclusive of all entertainment—there are no expensive extras.

**BUTLIN'S —**
*From Coast to Coast — the Nation's Host*

BUTLIN'S
Redcoat operating Radio B...

**BUTLIN'S BOGNOR REGIS**
Sunbathing Lawns

**BUTLIN'S MINEHEAD**
A Corner of the Beachcomber Bar

**BUTLIN'S MINEHEAD**
The Olde Tyme Ballroom

◁△ Butlin's distinctive style and characteristic approach to decor is apparent from the many colourful postcards issued in the 1960s and 1970s. In these images everyone always seems to be having a good time. Indeed, the messages on the postcards consistently say just that. They also hint at the range of activities: 'Been dancing tonight, donkey derby tomorrow.'

◁ An official Butlin's photographer captured these two, relaxing after one of the many themed evenings 'at one o'clock in the morning!', as it says on the back. Regular Butliners knew to take fancy dress clothes with them.

▷ 1930s chalets were very basic. This is Mollie, at Corton Holiday Camp in 1939. Within a few weeks Britain would be at war: most holiday camps closed for the duration, with many being taken over by the military.

# OUR CARAVAN HOLIDAY IN SELSEY — 1937

1. Well, here we are, after a good run down in the Morris. The caravan's not bad.

2. After tea, time for a smoke while washing out those smalls.

3. Robert 'enjoys' a cold wash while Thelma enjoys the joke.

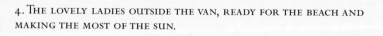

4. The lovely ladies outside the van, ready for the beach and making the most of the sun.

5. Robert and dad ready for a spin on the bike.

6. Last day and getting ready to load up the Morris. The dogs loved the trip.

# THE ISLE OF WIGHT

EMINENT VICTORIANS, notably Queen Victoria, Prince Albert and Lord Tennyson, made the Isle of Wight a fashionable resort, and the island's modern development dates from that era. Regular ferry services and, from the 1860s, its own railway network made it accessible to visitors, who enjoyed its diversity of landscape, coastal scenery and historic buildings. The island has retained many of the qualities that appealed to the Victorians, offering visitors a vision of an England long lost elsewhere.

unlimited travel
ISLE OF WIGHT
with HOLIDAY
RUNABOUT TICKETS

During 1961 Holiday Runabout Tickets in the Isle of Wight will be obtainable from 30th April to 27th October, available for six days, starting any day from SUNDAY to FRIDAY (but not valid on Saturdays)

They can be purchased at stations in the island for travel on any train between stations on the above map.

For the assistance of Holders of these tickets a time table of rail services (Sundays to Fridays) for the period 12th June to 10th September 1961 is given in this folder.

CHILDREN HALF PRICE
(3 years and under 14)

**10/-**
SECOND CLASS

BICYCLE 5/-
DOG
INVALID CHAIR
(Not folded) under 60 lb. in weight
PRAM (Not folded) 7/6
TANDEM

**15/-** FIRST CLASS

Transport Commission's published Regulations and Conditions charge at station booking offices

BRITISH RAILWAYS BOARD (S)
**ISLE OF WIGHT
HOLIDAY RUNABOUT TICKET**

2nd CLASS
Rate £-.10.0

VALID FROM    11 JUN 1965

UNTIL    17 JUN 1965

between the stations shown on back by the routes indicated
Agency No 4.9.D.
(5460)
Signature of holder    W H Askew

FOR CONDITIONS ENQUIRE AT TICKET OFFICE
This Ticket is NOT TRANSFERABLE and must be given up on expiry

NOT VALID FOR TRAVEL ON SATURDAYS
NOT VALID BEFORE 9.00 A.M. MONDAYS TO FRIDAYS

NOT VALID FOR TRAVEL ON SATURDAYS

No. T0001

◀ In the early 1960s regular ferry services to and from the mainland, and connections with the remains of the railway network, encouraged holidaymakers to visit the island.

▶ A long-established island joke is maintained by this 1960 card.

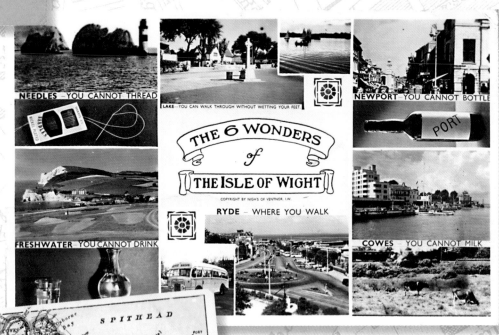

NEEDLES — YOU CANNOT THREAD

LAKE — YOU CAN WALK THROUGH WITHOUT WETTING YOUR FEET

NEWPORT — YOU CANNOT BOTTLE

PORT

THE 6 WONDERS
of
THE ISLE OF WIGHT
COPYRIGHT BY NIGH'S OF VENTNOR, I.W.
RYDE — WHERE YOU WALK

FRESHWATER — YOU CANNOT DRINK

COWES — YOU CANNOT MILK

**ISLE OF WIGHT
CAR FERRY
SERVICES
1962**

**PORTSMOUTH to FISHBOURNE
NEAR RYDE
LYMINGTON to YARMOUTH**

SOUTHERN
BRITISH RAILWAYS

▶ This Edwardian map card shows the island's railway network.

SPITHEAD

THE SOLENT

NEWPORT

ISLE · OF · WIGHT

Scale
0 1 2 3 4 Miles

Small Hope Beach, Shanklin, I.W.

▶ Mr Attrill's shell-covered house near East Cowes was a favourite sight.

MR ATTRILL AT WORK

*Photo. WHITE & SON, E. COWES*

SHELL HOUSE EAST COWES, I.W.

*Copyright Photo. WHITE & SON EAST COWES*

Russells

# WALKS & RAMBLES
# ISLE OF WIGHT

DIRECTIONS FOR SOME OF THE MOST PICTURESQUE WALKS IN THE ISLAND 1/6

▲ Many guides encouraged walkers to explore the island. This one dates from the early 1960s.

VENTNOR FROM THE EAST, ISLE OF WIGHT. 590

▲ Ventnor, on the south coast, was always a popular resort. The writer of this 1920 card says: 'The I. of W. is far above Harlech for scenery.'

▶ Ryde pier, one of the oldest in Britain, was for many the perfect introduction to the island.

◀ Beach huts and a mass of changing tents show the popularity of Shanklin.

RYDE, I.W.

**WHAT'S YOUR COLOUR?**

The fit of a Wolsey bathing suit can be seen at a glance. Look at the soft, springy wool. Look at the trim tailoring. All you need think about is colour and style. That's hard enough when you've so many suits to choose from, each more exciting than the last.

Picture what they'd look like on you, in the sea, on the sunshiny sand. Don't be rash, remember what a lot you'll want to wear it, but remember you don't have to wear it with anything, and choose your own pet colours.

The colours are fast to sea-water. The suits won't shrink and won't lose their shape. Prices are low. And it is worth remembering in these times that Wolsey bathing suits give employment to British people in Leicester.

# WOLSEY BATHING SUITS

WOLSEY LIMITED, LEICESTER

# WHAT
# WE WORE

*"Fashion is made
to become unfashionable."*

COCO CHANEL (1883–1971)

# OUT & ABOUT

IN THE LATE-VICTORIAN and Edwardian eras, holidays and day outings were both a novelty and something special. Everyone in photographs from that period looks unbelievably smart and sometimes, to our eyes, quite unsuitably dressed – especially the children. But good quality clothes, and plenty of them, were then the norm in everyday life. Hats were almost universally worn, and it was only the blazer and the straw hat that made any sort of gesture towards holiday dressing. These habits died hard, the smart approach lived on, and it was not until the 1950s that casual clothes, as we think of them, began to have any serious impact on holiday wear.

▽ This elderly man and his wife perfectly illustrate the Edwardian dress code for a day's outing. He is in a heavy tweed, three-piece suit, with wing collar and tie. She is wearing many layers, although the sun is shining, and carries a raincoat over her arm. Both have hats and sturdy, well-polished shoes.

◁ Four ladies out for a stroll along the promenade at Margate in the 1920s were captured by a beach photographer. The cloche hats and strappy shoes are the height of fashion, while the older lady's quilted satin coat is probably from an earlier era.

THE OLDER THE FIDDLE THE BETTER
THE TUNE.

◁ Excursions to the country were a common phenomenon in the early 1900s, especially for groups of work colleagues and members of church or similar societies. Typically, everyone in this group looks immaculately turned out.

△ It is hard to tell the players from the onlookers in this game, especially as no one is wearing bowling shoes, which were widely available by the 1920s, when this photograph was taken.

THEY ALL THINK I'M LORD NOZOO DOWN 'ERE.
Sûr qu'ils me prennent tous pour un grand seigneur
AT EASTBOURNE!

FREDᵏ SPURGIN

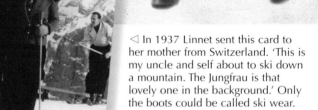

◁ In 1937 Linnet sent this card to her mother from Switzerland. 'This is my uncle and self about to ski down a mountain. The Jungfrau is that lovely one in the background.' Only the boots could be called ski wear.

△ This 1930s snap from a family album shows a mother with her son, in shorts and a splendid blazer, and daughter, carrying her Box Brownie camera, as they walk through a park in a seaside resort.

◁ The sailor suit was a perennial holiday favourite for children from the late-Victorian period onwards. This studio portrait, from about 1910, shows a whiter-than-white little sailor girl.

▷ A group of Edwardian ladies has paused for a cup of tea while on an excursion. One woman wears a fox fur, which, in those days, would not have seemed at all remarkable.

▷ This lively group striding along the promenade was recorded for posterity by a 1930s street photographer. The men wear their bathing costumes under their trousers, while the girls have set the holiday mood with halter-neck tops. The one on the left is in a smart linen suit, while the other has chosen a more casual look, with belted shorts.

# PANAMA HATS

*Despite its name, the Panama hat comes from Ecuador. When Teddy Roosevelt visited the Panama Canal, he wore such a hat, and the name has stuck. The prince of straw hats, the Panama has been associated with tropical elegance and seaside fun since the early 1900s. The best are made from the fibres of the Toquilla palm, quality depending upon the density of the weave. An ordinary hat might have 100 weaves per square inch, but the finest have up to 2,000 and cost several thousand dollars. The test of a Panama is whether it holds water and can be folded without damage. The best can be rolled and fitted into a cigar tube.*

PANAMA HATS ON THEIR WAY THROUGH THE GATUN LOCKS TO MADURO'S SOUVENIR STORE.

△ A Penzance street photographer spotted this couple on holiday in 1952. The man, in particular, is in holiday mode, wearing a casual shirt with open collar, an old sports jacket, baggy trousers and a beret.

△ Two couples enjoy a picnic in a park somewhere in Britain in the 1930s. Their clothes are relatively formal, with the men in suits and ties, but there is a definite holiday atmosphere.

▷ This photograph shows 'Mr Chester, the Scoutmaster, and his car', presumably taken on a Scouts holiday sometime in the 1930s. There is an air of informality in the mix of uniform and old tweed jacket.

# WHEN TAKING A WALK

## Dressmaker Suits and Slip-on Coats for the Promenade

EACH of these designs is modelled in 32, 34, 36, 38 and 40-in. bust sizes. Pattern No. 11,819 costs 1s. 3d. all other designs are priced at 1s. 6d. each—every pattern plus 1d. extra to cover postage. Please send your order to The Pattern Shop, at the address on page 3.

Bolero and Skirt
No. 11,872

(Left)
No. 11,842 A

(Left)
Suit
No. 11,937

(Right)
Jigger Coat
No. 11,819

Two-Way Cardigan Suit
No. 11,842 A & B

No. 11,842 B

No. 11,842 A and B.
UNUSUALLY chic and ideal for Summer wear is the new sleeveless cardigan suit. Made in a tubbable fabric, it will look incredibly smart in white pique or near-linen over a strongly contrasting shirt blouse—black, if you like, teamed up with a scarlet handbag. If you feel that your Summer wardrobe is sufficiently stocked, then make it with sleeves in a light woollen fabric, the jacket lined for additional warmth. Allow 4½ yds. of 36-in. or 2½ yds. of 54-in. for the sleeved model ; 3½ yds. of 36-in., if sleeveless. Lining for the jacket takes 2 yds. of 36-in. (with sleeves) or 1½ yds. without. Add ⅝ yd. of inch-wide petersham.

No. 11,872.
IT'S not the smartest models which have the most work in them ; nine times out of ten chic depends entirely on the simplicity of the cut and designing. As with the bolero and built-up skirt above—the latter dependent on a shaped under-waistband (canvas lined) for its perfect fit and line. For Summer wear make it from 3½ yds. of 36-in. spun rayon—for cooler days 2½ yds. of 54-in. woollen. Bolero lining takes 1½ yds. of 36-in., in either case, and canvas interlining ½ yd. in a 27-in. width.

No. 11,937.
A VERY up-to-date design, which is figure flattering and slimming in the extreme. And the simplicity of the making has to be experienced to be believed, for the underarm seams are left untouched until jacket fronts and back are seamed (epaulettes included), so that you can do all your piecing together flat on the table. Allow 2½ yds. of 54-in. material, 2 yds. of 36-in. lining and ⅝ yd. of 1-in. petersham.

No. 11,819.
A CASUAL swinging coat is worth its weight in gold when wardrobes are scanty. Excellent over Summer dresses, it partners cardigan suit or slim woollen frock right through the Spring and Autumn days, looks well with tweeds, teams up with slacks. Make up in a gay smooth woollen, allowing 1½ yds. of 54-in. material and 2½ yds. of 36-in. lining. Or, if coupons are scarce, line shoulders and sleeves from ⅛ yd.

△◁ This late-1930s edition of Leach-Way Holiday Wear is typical of the many publications of that era aimed at those who made their own clothes. Each page has its own theme: 'Holiday Essentials', 'Seashore Clothes in a Lively Mood', 'Tailored or Frilled', 'Girls' Holiday Frocks', and (left) 'When Taking a Walk'.

△ This girl is obviously pleased with her classic 1950s-style dress, all tight waist and full skirt in an exotic palm tree and canoe pattern. She probably made it herself.

# ON THE BEACH

FASHIONS IN BEACHWEAR have changed dramatically over the last hundred years, and clothes worn in the past by highly fashionable men and women look extraordinary, eccentric and even entertaining. In general, there has been a steady shift from the voluminous and modest to the skimpy and revealing, with the result that the way people once dressed for a day at the seaside often seems nothing short of amazing.

"SAY, OFFICER, IF THOSE GALS CAN RUN ROUND IN PYJAMAS, WHY D'YER PINCH ME FOR COMIN' OUT IN ME NIGHTSHIRT?"

△ This shows Mother and Susan the dog on Thorpeness beach, in Suffolk, probably in the early 1920s. In the days when pale skin, rather than a suntan, was desirable, Mother follows convention by keeping herself covered up and using an umbrella as a sunshade.

△ A large family spending a day at the seaside has assembled for a photograph. Two of the girls have been digging in the sand and there are two deckchairs, but the 1930s clothes seem unbelievably inappropriate: suits, hats, smart frocks, a winter coat, a fox fur. Even the boy looks ready for church rather than the beach. Yet this is not unusual, and similar images are to be found in many family albums from the Edwardian era to the 1930s.

◁ Two women pose in similar beachwear. The long beach dress, or costume, was a legacy of the time when public bathing was segregated. By the 1920s, when this photograph was taken, the garment was much less cumbersome, but still designed with modesty in mind.

▽ Anyone of a certain age remembers the hand-knitted bathing costume, and how soggy and saggy it was when wet. This little girl wears a Mickey Mouse version, at Swanage in 1951, but there were numerous variations for doting mums or grannies to choose from. The pattern below is for a matching sun suit and cardigan, in Lister's Lavenda wool.

HOME FASHIONS No.11
# HOLIDAY CLOTHES

4½d

N°1046

4d

FREE PATTERN

FREE PATTERN

BARGAIN PATTERN

BARGAIN PATTERN
for this
FRILLY FROCK

CANNOT BE EXCHANGED.

Hand Knitwear in Lavenda

...TERNS for PINK & WHITE 2-PIECE & WHITE FROCK
Inside

◁ In the Victorian and Edwardian eras, ladies preserved their decency by wearing loose-fitting costumes. Typical is this two-piece example, with its fancy trimming. Fairly shapeless when dry, such costumes must have looked extraordinary when wet.

▷ Until the 1960s it was quite normal to make your own clothes. The guide to holiday fashions (top right) is from 1939, but many of the styles were still popular for several years after World War II. The girls in this beach group (right) seem to have used just such a guide.

◁ This handsome couple on Sheringham beach, Norfolk, were probably fashion icons in 1935. Her costume is certainly à la mode, and she sports the fitted rubber swimming cap. His woollen costume would, of course, be even more revealing after a bathe in the sea.

▷ This 1930s beach dandy's combination of tight trunks, cricket sweater, cravat, sunglasses and colourful beach ball is a seaside classic, and the ultimate fashion statement.

"Look, daddy,—that poor lady didn't have any moth balls, did she?"

△ Two smiling girls, in model pose, show off the latest in USA-style 1950s beachwear.

◁ Gertrude is having a lovely time on her beach holiday in 1954, posing here in a strapless bathing costume that would have been chosen for sunbathing rather than energetic swimming.

△ This is seaside paddling 1950s style, with full skirts hitched up or tucked into knickers and baggy trousers rolled up above the knee.

▷ Amateur fashion parades were a feature of beach life in 1950s and early 1960s Britain. These ladies are strutting their stuff in one of a series of holiday fashion shows organized at regional resorts by a national newspaper.

△ In 1932 beach pyjamas were the latest thing, with Hollywood musicals setting the standard. These jolly girls have done their best to catch the style with limited resources but plenty of imagination.

△ This carefully posed photograph of an early 1920s swimming team, perhaps enjoying a day on the beach during a tour in the school holidays, shows off the latest style in ladies' swimwear.

71

# OUR HOLIDAY IN WALES – 1935

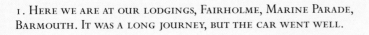

1. HERE WE ARE AT OUR LODGINGS, FAIRHOLME, MARINE PARADE, BARMOUTH. IT WAS A LONG JOURNEY, BUT THE CAR WENT WELL.

2. A HOT DAY FOR AN OUTING AND THE LADIES HAVE SETTLED DOWN FOR A PICNIC – SOME FRUIT AND A CUP OF TEA. SHOES HAVE BEEN CAST OFF!

3. WE SAW OUR FILL OF WATERFALLS AROUND BETWS-Y-COED.

④

⑥

⑤

⑦

4. It was a cold day but we couldn't resist this spot for another picnic. The flat rock made a perfect table.

5. Barmouth — wonderful weather and wonderful sands at low tide.

6. We had a good time at Carnarvon Castle.

7. An unusual encounter in the pass above Tal-y-Llyn.

# LLANDUDNO

SPREAD AROUND THE WIDE BAY between the headlands of Great Orme and Little Orme, Llandudno is one of the most famous resorts on the North Wales coast. The town was largely a development of the Victorian era, laid out as a new resort by Edward Mostyn and Owen Williams, who chose the site because of its two beaches, west and east of the Great Orme. Rapid growth, encouraged by the opening of the branch railway from Llandudno Junction, brought many hotels to the resort, and it became known as a centre for exploring Snowdonia. From 1902, climbing the 679 feet to the summit of the Great Orme was made easier by a cable car railway, the only one of its kind in Britain.

LLANDUDNO BAY

▲ This 1920s card shows the wide sweep of the bay from the Great Orme to the Little Orme.

The Pier & Old Toll Gate, Llandudno.

► The pier, shown here on a 1906 card, was part of Llandudno's Victorian development.

▼ Llandudno has always offered plenty to satisfy visitors, including a town band.

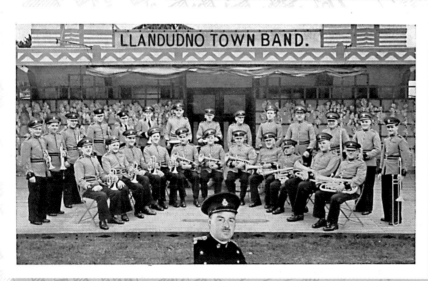

LLANDUDNO TOWN BAND.

► Llandudno featured early in Ward Lock's well-known series of 'red guides'. This edition dates from the 1950s.

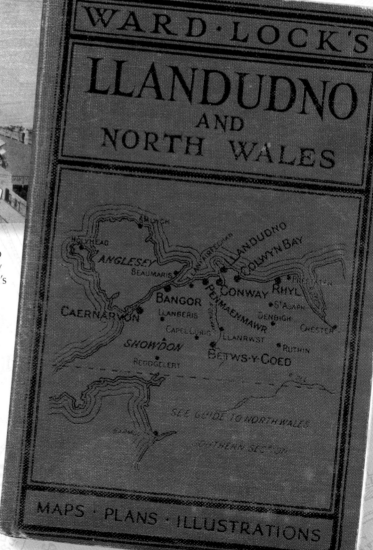

WARD·LOCK'S
LLANDUDNO
AND
NORTH WALES

MAPS · PLANS · ILLUSTRATIONS

HISTORIC CONWAY
SUNNY DEGANWY AND
LLANDUDNO JUNCTION

Price 3D.

L. & N. W. RY.
Llandudno

HAVE GOT AIRY APARTMENTS AT LLANDUDNO

▲ Every resort has its own comic cards. This one was posted in 1910.

◄▲ It was the railway that brought most visitors to Llandudno, and enabled them to see other places of interest in the region. The guidebook is an early 1960s example.

▲ This hand-coloured Edwardian photograph shows Happy Valley, an area of Llandudno always popular with visitors. A minstrel band is playing to a large crowd.

Two De Luxe Modes of Travel,
CLYNO OLYMPIC SALOON & WHITE STAR LINE R.M.S OLYMPIC.

# TOURING

"*For my part, I travel not to go anywhere, but to go. I travel for travel's sake. The great affair is to move.*"

ROBERT LOUIS STEVENSON (1850–1894)

# BY COACH

It was during the 1920s, as motor vehicles became more reliable, faster and much more comfortable, that outings in open-top charabancs became popular. By the 1930s coach companies were offering all-in touring holidays, lasting one or two weeks. At the same time, a network of scheduled long-distance coach services spread throughout Britain, in competition with the railways. After World War II the coach business grew enormously, again thanks to better vehicles and roads, and since then the luxury coach tour has been a vital part of the holiday industry.

"NO MORE CHARABANC TRIPS FOR ME—EVERY MINUTE I THOUGHT I'D BE HURLED INTO MATERNITY!"

▽ The first charabancs were mostly slow, noisy, fairly uncomfortable and had only rudimentary wet-weather cover. Groups were regularly photographed before setting off, and these images offer a wonderful insight into the early days of coach travel. This party is about to depart from London, in the 1920s, in a solid-tyred vehicle owned by Albert Ewer. Only the driver seems prepared for the rigours of the journey.

By sea and mountain loch and glen

◁ In the 1950s the coach industry greatly improved its image, and touring holidays were promoted as convenient and luxurious. This delightful drawing, advertising coach touring in Scotland, shows a streamlined vehicle and a fashionable young couple enjoying the comfort and the panoramic views. Smoking was, of course, allowed!

△ Passengers board a classic 1950s coach operated by Cream Cars. The aerodynamic shape, the two-tone finish and the gleaming chrome are characteristic of the period, as are the crew's smart, maritime-style uniforms.

△ This photograph shows a typical late 1950s group assembled outside a hotel in Scotland and clearly having good fun on a Wallace Arnold tour.

△ A more informal group of the same era poses with the Venney's coach driver, also in fairly casual dress, by one of the highlights of the day's scenic tour.

# TOURING BRITAIN BY COACH

◁▽ This Travel Association brochure promoted touring holidays and scheduled long-distance services operated by the coach industry, including Associated Motorways' day and night services. Many local and regional bus companies also expanded into the coach touring business, a typical example being Hants and Dorset Motor Services.

△ Many remote areas suffered from the railway closures of the early 1960s. One solution tried in Scotland and Wales was the post bus, which combined passenger-carrying with postal services. This 1960s example is at Abbey Cwmhir, Powys.

*With the Compliments of*

## HANTS AND DORSET

### MOTOR SERVICES LTD

*Pavilion Garage*
*8 Bath Road*
*Bournemouth*

FROM
TOURIST COACH STATION,
1, GROSVENOR SQUARE,
SOUTHAMPTON

REGULAR DAY & NIGHT SERVICES

to all parts of
**SOUTH WALES AND WEST OF ENGLAND**
ALSO DAILY SERVICES
MIDLANDS *to* SOUTH COAST

ASSOCIATED MOTORWAYS
REGULAR SERVICES

BY LUXURY COACHES FROM VICTORIA COACH STATION
ASSOCIATED MOTORWAYS, HEAD OFFICE: COACH STATION, CHELTENHAM

▽ There is snow on the ground on a cold winter's day in Scarborough in the late 1930s. These passengers are well wrapped up, especially the ladies, and they are all looking cheerful as they pose in front of the fleet of three Crosbys coaches, ready for whatever the day will bring.

△ In the 1950s an all-male group poses for a picture before boarding the coach. The men are clearly out for a good time and, with a piano accordion and banjo on board, there is sure to be singing en route.

▽ The vicar is sitting in the centre of this 1930s group, so this is probably a church outing, and since, apart from the vicar and the driver, there is only one man present, it could well be the Mothers' Union.

# BY TRAIN

RAILWAYS HAVE RUN excursion trains since the 1840s, and the involvement of railways in the holiday business is almost as old. In order to encourage traffic on their ever-expanding networks, railway companies built ports and harbours, operated steamers and hotels, and helped to develop coastal and inland resorts all over Britain. Railways remained the prime mover for holiday traffic until the late 1960s.

▷ In summer many major stations were continually busy with holiday traffic. This is Paddington in the 1930s, with the Cornish Riviera Express about to depart.

△ A highlight of a journey on a holiday express was a visit to the dining car. This is a menu on a Great Western Railway express to Cornwall in the 1930s.

▷ In a gloriously evocative but wonderfully posed studio photograph from the GWR's publicity department in the 1930s, this couple prepare to leave the train at the start of their holiday.

# EXPLORE
## THE SOUTH COAST
### WITH A
## DAY TOUR TICKET

AND ENJOY
### A DAY'S UNLIMITED TRAVEL

**9'6** AREA **34**
SECOND CLASS

**8'6** AREA **35**
SECOND CLASS

CHILDREN 3 and UNDER 14 YEARS HALF PRICE

SUNDAYS to FRIDAYS 29 APRIL to 28 OCTOBER
INCLUSIVE

DAY TOUR TICKETS ARE ON SALE AT ANY STATION OR TRAVEL AGENCY
IN THE AREAS SHOWN OVERLEAF. THEY ARE AVAILABLE FOR TRAVEL
BY ANY TRAIN ON THE DAY OF ISSUE WITHIN THE AREA SELECTED

SOUTHERN    A SUPPLEMENTARY CHARGE IS MADE FOR TRAVEL IN PULLMAN CARS

# HOLIDAY
## RUNABOUT
## TICKETS

h April to 31st October 1953

### UNLIMITED TRAVEL
in the areas and for the periods shown

ates from 10/6 third class

FULL DETAILS CAN BE OBTAINED ON
ARRIVAL AT YOUR DESTINATION

BRITISH RAILWAYS

D.147/H.D.
## COMBINED RAIL
## AND ROAD TRIP

SUNDAY 30th JUNE
TO
# DOVEDALE
In conjunction with the Trent Motor Traction Co.

**14/6**
Inclusive
Second Class
Return Fare

Rail to Derby
and

Children three and under fourteen years

BIRMINGHAM New
Depart 11.45 a.m.

ITINERARY OF TOUR

DESCRIPTION OF ROAD TOUR

SPECIAL NOTICE

DOGS ARE NOT CONVEYED ON THE ROAD TOURS

LONDON MIDLAND

# SUNDAY
## EXCURSIONS

FROM
## PADDINGTON
AND
## EALING BROADWAY
DURING
## MAY, 1955

Paddington Station, W.2.
March, 1955.

BRITISH RAILWAYS

TRAVEL

£1
5/-

MID-WEEK

save up to 5/- in the £1

BRITISH RAILWAYS

◁ △ ▷ The running of
excursions had long been an
important part of the railway
passenger business, but during
the 1950s and 1960s British
Railways made special efforts
to hold on to this, faced
as it was with increasing
competition from coaches and
private cars. Many things were
tried, including the promotion
of off-peak and weekend
travel, day and week runabout
tickets, and special combined
rail and coach excursions
to areas that were not easily
accessible by train alone. To
make the leaflets promoting
these services attractive,
a range of highly varied,
adventurous and entertaining
graphic effects were used,
many of which retain a
delightful period quality.

# A TRIP TO LONDON

As a CAPITAL CITY, London has always, for much of the population of Britain, been easily accessible, and has long been seen as the ideal destination for a day out or a short break. Offering something for everyone, from museums and galleries, music and theatre to parks and gardens, restaurants and cafés, department stores and street markets, a visit to London was a perennially popular choice for a special celebration or a family treat in the school holidays.

▽ Posing with the pigeons in Trafalgar Square was an essential part of any London visit in the 1950s. These three, probably in town for the day, are making the most of a classic photo opportunity.

▷ This Edwardian postcard, from a series called 'Our Belles', entertainingly uses pictures of pretty girls in bell-shaped mounts to frame a view of Tower Bridge with its bascules open. In the foreground a pleasure steamer and a sailing barge approach the bridge.

◁▽ A pair of classic 1950s postcards show classic London views. The one of Trafalgar Square has a strange message: 'How would you like to be with Nelson on the top of his column? A trifle cold and the pigeons might be a nuisance.'

TRAFALGAR SQUARE

A TUCK CARD

EROS, PICCADILLY CIRCUS, LONDON.

▷▽ Visitors had a vast choice of day trips and weekend breaks, many organized by British Railways. Events for the day tripper in the 1962/3 winter season included the National School Boys' Own Exhibition, the International Radio Hobbies Exhibition, the Furniture Exhibition and the Royal Dairy Show.

RL 6289

(S7F) London Passenger Transport Board (Tramways)

2d Wk   33 48 78

Return Journey only Change at Brixton Station

C | Change Brixton (Gresham Rd) Camberwell Gate and Swan, Stockwell
Camberwell Green and Tate Library | Loughborough Junction and Vauxhall Stn.

1 Southampton Row | Waterloo Br. (Savoy St.) 2
2 Farringdon Road (Rosebery Avenue) | Westminster Station 3
3 Angel | Victoria 3
4 North | York Road Christchurch or Regency St. 4
5 Balls Pond Rd Midway Pk | Fitzalan Street or Vauxhall Station 5
6 Albion Road | Kennington Gate or The Library 6
7 Lordship Park | Angell Road or Swan Stockwell 7
8 Manor House | Brixton Stn (Acre Ln. or Stockwell Rd.) 8
12 Norwood | Dalberg Road 9
11 Tulse Hill | City (via Southwark) 3
10 Croxted Road | St George's Church 4
9 Jessop Road |
8 Loughboro' Junction |
7 Camberwell Green |
6 Camberwell Gate | Elephant 5

For conditions see back

XM 5018

4

LONDON TRANSPORT BUSES

Available to point indicated by the punch-hole and must be shown on demand. NOT TRANSFERABLE

1 26
2 25
3 24
4 23
5 22
6 21
7 20
8 19
9 18
10 17
11 16
12 15
13 14

▷ A visit to the Tower of London, with its colourful Beefeaters, was on every visitor's list.

LONDON - BUCKINGHAM PALACE AND QUEEN VICTORIA MEMORIAL.

△ Another classic postcard of the 1950s shows Buckingham Palace, where the Changing of the Guard was always popular.

# BY CAR & MOTORCYCLE

BEFORE WORLD WAR I cars were expensive and roads were poor, so the touring holiday did not really get going until the 1920s. During the next two decades, as reliability improved and prices dropped, car and motorcycle ownership became more common. By the 1960s the family car was part of the normal household and was used for holidays. Journeys were facilitated by better roads, including the first motorways.

▽ Somewhere in the Cotswolds these two ladies are studying the map, deciding where to head for in their smart new Austin A30. This card was from a series issued by Austin to promote their range in the 1950s. It described the A30 as 'a 4-door saloon with lively performance and extra-economical running'.

▷ These two large ladies in their summer frocks are having a great time sitting on a big Matchless touring motorcycle. They probably won't go far beyond this layby, where they were photographed in the 1950s, but they look ready for anything.

HOLIDAY TOURS BY CAR

SMITH'S POTATO CRISPS

The Lake District

See that SMITH'S CRISPS are always included in your picnic basket

◁ Maps and guides were issued from the 1930s to encourage car touring. Most were produced by petrol companies, but there were many other manufacturers, including Smith's, then the most famous name in crisps.

△ Two sports cars are parked outside a grand house or hotel somewhere in 1930s England. The cars are clean, polished, and ready for a day out in the country. Perhaps some unofficial road racing is about to take place, with short odds on the Morgan.

◁ It is 1926 and several cars are parked by a beach near Torquay. These young people are posing in front of the grand touring car parked above them, probably the property of the man in plusfours.

△ Sitting on the car bonnet, astride the radiator temperature gauge, was a favourite pose for girls in the 1930s. This particular one was photographed during a touring holiday in the West Country.

When the first motorways were opened in Britain in the late 1950s, they were such a novelty that people drove along them for pleasure. Even more exciting were the first motorway service stations. These proved to be so popular that postcards of them were put on sale. These two show the dramatic 1960s architecture and the spacious and elegant interior, complete with designer chairs, of the Forton Service Area, on the M6, in Lancashire.

PENNINE TOWER RESTAURANT

S.1120

△ The biking gear might suggest that these two girls have been riding this 1950s Triumph motorcycle. However, a learner with L-plates could not carry a pillion passenger, so maybe it was just a dress rehearsal.

▽ Three ladies, in classic tweeds, pose beside a new Morris Minor. Perhaps it is being run in on a gentle touring holiday.

Having a ripping time at PLYMOUTH

◁ It is August 1927 and this enterprising photographer has taken one of his studio props, an ancient motorcycle and sidecar, down to the beach. This family has seized the chance of a make-believe journey.

▽ This rather extraordinary 1930s family album photograph is captioned 'The Goods'. Mr Good has taken a break from the driving and, cigar in hand, sits uncompromisingly in front of his grand touring car with its racy mascot. The women will not be allowed a turn at driving.

△ BSA was one of the great names in British motorcycling, at its peak in the 1950s, when this catalogue was issued. At that time the company produced more than 12 models, ranging in price from £94 to £252. Many were designed for the kind of cross-country touring illustrated so evocatively on the cover.

△ It seems to have been a tradition in the 1920s and 1930s for ladies to be photographed astride motorcycles they probably did not own. This young flapper may have been able to ride the BSA, but she is hardly dressed for it.

▷ In the mid-1920s two families are on holiday, or perhaps on a day out, in the country. The old tourer may have seen better days, but clearly the young girl in the blazer loved her ride in the dickey seat in the back.

THE HOMELAND GUIDE TO
THE LAKE DISTRICT

2/6

AN ENTIRELY NEW GUIDE
With Footpath Walks

NATIONAL
BENZOLE
BOOKS

Philips' Series of Map Guides : No. 2

London's
Countryside

Showing the
New Arterial
Roads

A
MAP-GUIDE
FOR THE
Antiquarian,
Tourist &
Sportsman.

PRICE
1/-
NET

GEORGE PHILIP & SON, LIMITED
32 FLEET STREET, E.C.4

Follies

6s

National

EDITOR SIR HUGH CASSON

△▷ As the use of cars for leisure purposes increased, maps and guides proliferated. These were produced by established map and guidebook publishers and by others with motoring connections, such as petrol companies. These examples date from the 1920s to the 1960s.

# IN A CAMPERVAN

In the early days, motorized caravans were individually designed and built or were adapted from existing vehicles. In its simplest form, a conventional caravan was mounted on the back of a flatbed lorry. The factory-built motorized caravan did not emerge in its current form until the late 1950s, by which time there was a wide range of van-type vehicles that could be used as a base. The campervan, as it became known, was usually produced by specialized makers working with vehicle manufacturers, and more and more became available during the 1960s.

△▷ The Dormobile was a two- or four-berth vehicle, based on a Ford Thames van. Developed by Martin Walter of Folkestone, it is lavishly illustrated in this 1962 brochure. Included in the price of just over £800 were a kitchen with gas-fired rings and grill, a dining area, a chemical toilet and an elevating roof. The interior was finished in 'grey mahogany melamine veneer', and curtains were supplied.

The World Famous Ford Thames Dormobile Motorised Caravan

**TWO AND FOUR BERTH MODELS**

## "The World is Your Oyster"

Go where you like
— there are seats for six

Stay where you like
— there are beds for four

Eat where you like
— there's a 'diner' too

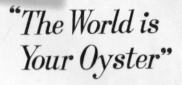

*Martin Walter Ltd*

Estd. 1773

**DORMOBILE WORKS FOLKESTONE, ENGLAND**

◁ Another popular model was the Commer Caravan, shown in this delightful drawing in the 1961 brochure with a view of the interior – 'a triumph of space planning' – and the 'ingenious elevating roof'.

▽ The iconic campervan of the 1960s was the VW Camper. This version is the Devonette, designed and made by White's of Sidmouth, and displayed in a classic family setting. The table is laid for tea, and mum, dad and the little girl amuse themselves while the boy brings water for the kettle.

## FISH & CHIPS

*Fish & chips is the classic British take-away meal. The spread of the railways in the late 1800s meant that low-cost fish – hitherto thrown back into the sea because it had no market – could be carried swiftly inland. Cheap fried fish became a staple food of the working classes. They looked for it when away on holiday too, and soon there were chippies in every holiday resort. Traditionally, fish & chips was wrapped in newspaper, which kept the heat in and allowed the steam to soften the food slightly, giving it its distinctive smell, flavour and texture.*

THE END OF A PERFECT DAY! AT LLANDUDNO

# OUR GIRL GUIDES SUMMER CAMP – 1937

1. HERE WE ARE ARRIVING, AFTER THE LONG WALK FROM THE STATION. THE GIRLS WHO CAME ON THE LORRY WITH THE LUGGAGE WERE JOLLY LUCKY!

2. GETTING THE TENTS UP IS ALWAYS A BIT OF A BATTLE.

3. RAISING THE FLAG! ATTENTION GIRLS (AND LET'S HOPE THE UNION JACK IS THE RIGHT WAY UP).

4. Get those fires burning, we're famished! Quick, more wood!

5. Spud-bashing squad at work.

6. Water-carrying detail — the worst job in the camp.

7. In the dorm! Lights out, girls, and stop talking!

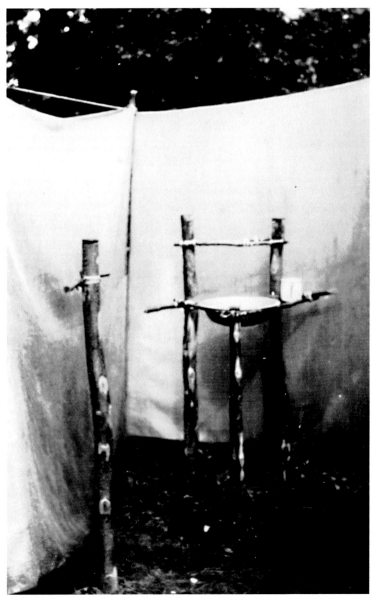

8. Our super de luxe bathroom!

9. Pow-wow and sing-song. All together, girls!

10. A bit of first aid. Nurse, pass that scalpel!

11

13

12

14

11. Picnic on the beach — and didn't it taste good!

12. Even the washing up was fun.

13. Gym on the beach. What a super day that was!

14. It's all over and here we are back at the station. Smile, girls!

# DERBYSHIRE DALES

THE LANDSCAPE OF DERBYSHIRE and the Peak District was first appreciated in the 18th century, thanks to artists such as Joseph Wright. By the Victorian period, with access made easier by the railways, the region began to enjoy a much greater popularity, particularly around the spa towns of Buxton and Matlock. In the mid-20th century, with the spread of walking and outdoor pursuits, the quality of the area's landscape was fully recognized when the Peak District National Park was established.

▲ The splendid landscape, and youth hostel, of Castleton feature on this 1930s card.

◀▼ These two Edwardian cards show the famously remote Cat and Fiddle Inn in its moorland setting.

▲ The Derbyshire volume in Penguin's distinctive series of regional guides was published in 1939.

# THE PEAK DISTRICT

▲ This 1962 British Railways leaflet encouraged exploration by train.

▶ In the 1960s the region's 16 youth hostels were always popular.

BRITISH RAILWAYS

*Peak District Hostels*

◀ This 1904 card shows a typically artistic vision of High Tor, Matlock.

▶ An early hand-coloured postcard depicts the old bridge at Ashford-in-the-Water.

Derbyshire Dales.
Bridge at Ashford-in-the Water.

▲ The London & North Western Railway published this card of Isaac Walton's house to encourage train travel to the Dales.

NEWQUAY GWR
ON THE CORNISH COAST

# AT THE SEASIDE

*"I do like to be beside the seaside!*
*Oh, I do like to be beside the sea!"*

BY JOHN A GLOVER-KIND (1907)

# 'ALONG THE PROM, PROM, PROM'

A stroll along the prom is, as the popular song says, a highlight of any seaside holiday. It was in the late 1700s that the habit of parading along the front began. King George III led the parade at Weymouth, and other smart people, trying out the new fashion for sea bathing, followed suit at resorts such as Margate and Brighton. By the late-Victorian period the parade had become the promenade, a carefully constructed pathway above the beach that sometimes, as at Blackpool, stretched for miles. The prom was, and is, a place for taking the air, for seeing and being seen, for shops, entertainment and ice cream.

"View of the Sea from the Promenade!"

◁ A seaside photographer caught this family walking along the promenade, enjoying the sunshine, in the Silver Jubilee Year of 1935.

SILVER JUBILEE 1935. Sunny Snaps.

▷ In Teignmouth, Devon, in the summer of 1939, everyone is out on the promenade, and smart clothes are the order of the day. It looks windy, but this elegant threesome are prepared for all weathers.

# I enjoy walking along the Front.

▷ This delightful image of a happy young girl with her spotted headscarf and Japanese sunshade is actually a postcard from the 1920s. With her towel, bucket and spade, she is parading her dolls along the promenade, on her way to the beach.

△ Anticipating Bert Hardy's iconic 1950s *Picture Post* photograph of two girls sitting on the promenade railings, their skirts flying in the wind, this cheery but rather more modest pair adopt similar poses in the early 1920s.

△ It is obviously a chilly day in Brighton in July 1962, but these jolly ladies are still having fun. And, once they have escaped from the clutches of the artificial donkey, there's shopping to be done.

# ALL ABOARD!

THE DOUBLE-DECKED, open-top bus was a familiar sight throughout much of the Victorian era, and the motor bus, which came into widespread use in the Edwardian period, followed the same form. It was not until the 1920s that upper decks were regularly enclosed. By then the open-top bus had begun its long association with the seaside. Elderly buses were often sent from the cities to a retirement by the sea, where, much to the delight of the bus spotter, the combination of short seasons and brief journeys gave them many more years of service. Seaside buses were often converted from enclosed vehicles; others were custom-built.

△ This Edwardian card, sent from St Leonard's-on-Sea, in Sussex, shows a typical omnibus of the period, its upper deck filled with passengers enjoying the sunshine and the views as they eagerly await their ride along the seafront to the marina.

▽ There were not many takers for the circular tour to Ainsdale Beach on the day, in the 1960s, when this elderly Leyland bus was photographed in Southport, Lancashire.

△ Seaside buses have long lives. This 40-year-old veteran was still earning its keep and allowing plenty of people to enjoy the view from the open deck when photographed on the Isle of Wight.

▷ In a glorious evocation of the Edwardian era, a smartly dressed group, all boaters, blazers, fancy hats and white summer dresses, poses beside a London omnibus in about 1912, prior to a special outing, perhaps a family celebration.

PL 8324
2ᴰ
Westwards | Eastwards
Montague Place
Castle Square or Brighton Station | HOVE & PRESTON COMPANY, LIMITED.
York

I 0873
HASTINGS
Tramways Company.
PARCEL
Memorial | 5ᴰ
London Road | Devonshire Place
London Road | Metropole Hotel
Bopeep | No. 1 Fare Section Cooden
| No. 2 Fare Section Cooden
Bexhill Rd Fare Sec. | Cooden Terminus

Bp 1973
HANTS & DORSET
Motor Services, Ltd.
Issued subject to Regulations in Time Table. This ticket to be shown on demand.
Push Chair; Dog X
SINGLE
STAGE No. | SHIL'S PENCE

◁ Connections between the station and the beach were always important. Here, in 1950s Essex, a local Westcliff-on-Sea single-decker waits outside Southend station.

105

# PIERS

THE SEASIDE PLEASURE PIER seems to be a particularly British phenomenon. Initially piers were built as landing stages for paddle steamers bringing holidaymakers to the new seaside resorts in the early 1800s. Ideal walkways for enjoying the sea air, many later provided restaurants, theatres and other amusements. The first pier opened at Ryde, on the Isle of Wight, in 1814, and is still in use. The first cast-iron pier was built at Gravesend, Kent, in 1834, spawning a proliferation of similar piers around the coast. Now 55 survive in England and Wales. Others have been lost in storms, hit by ships, removed for defence reasons during World War II or simply allowed to decay.

▷ This view of Morecambe pier was sent in 1917 to a Miss Olive Preston by her grandfather. His message to her is: 'We are quite well. Tell your mama that she will attend to laundry.'

*Promenade and Bay, Morecambe*

*Bournemouth from Pier*

◁ By 1911, when this card was posted, Bournemouth was a highly fashionable South Coast resort and the pier was both elegant and well equipped, as can be seen.

HAVN'T GOT A BITE YET—BUT THE BAIT'S ALL RIGHT, AND THEY'RE NIBBLING!

▷ Redcar's pier, in North Yorkshire, was long, basic and bleak. Hit several times by ships during the late 1800s, it was finally demolished in 1981 after storm damage.

PROMENADE PIER, DOVER.

◁ In the Edwardian era, long before its development as a ferry port, Dover was still a smart resort, with a somewhat functional but not unattractive pier. This postcard was sent to Emmie by her father, who predictably writes: 'Hoping to hear you have been a good girl.'

▷▽ When, in about 1905, the Great Eastern Railway published its card (far right) to promote 'the most popular resort on the East Coast', Yarmouth's Winter Pavilion on the Britannia pier was a new and handsome attraction. After two world wars the Pavilion Theatre was still going strong in the 1950s, as this programme indicates. *Keep 'Em Laughing* was a typical seaside variety show, featuring comedy duo Jewel and Warriss, and dance band singer Anne Shelton. The card reproduced below shows that by the 1970s there have been changes: the Britannia Theatre still offers a nightly revue, but entertainment also takes the form of bingo and a chimps' tea party. Buildings cover the pier, and the elegance of the old theatre has been lost.

## BRITANNIA PIER

6ᴰ

### PAVILION THEATRE

GENERAL MANAGER FOR
NEW BRITANNIA PIER CO.          BRYAN MEREDITH

★

#### TOM ARNOLD'S
GREAT SEASON SHOW
#### KEEP 'EM LAUGHING

JIMMY          BEN
## JEWEL ᴬⁿᴰ WARRISS

ᴬᴺᴰ
GUEST STAR
## ANNE SHELTON

**NEW BRITANNIA PIER** GREAT YARMOUTH

Change of Programme Every Thursday
To-night

EVERY SUNDAY EVENING at 7.30
**NEVILLE BISHOP & HIS ORCHESTRA**
in a HAPPY-GO-LUCKY CONCERT

THE BRITANNIA PIER, GT YARMOUTH.

# SHOW TIME

PIER THEATRES HAVE LONG been a popular home for variety, and for well over a century they have competed to put on the most attractive programmes during the long summer season. Resident troupes, travelling groups and individual variety performers of all kinds fill the bill around visiting star turns, who from the 1950s were drawn increasingly from radio and television. Among all the variety, there is a certain consistency: for years Pierrot groups and black-and-white minstrels were popular, while many shows were described simply as 'Fol-de-Rols'. Sometimes an entire play was wrapped around the variety performers, like winter pantomime.

▷▽ Pier programmes are very diverse and appealing. Here, two come from Bournemouth: the *Star Light Roof* show of 1963, featuring Lance Percival, Winifred Atwell and Ronnie Carroll, and the 1964 risqué variety play *Camp Beds*, starring Thora Hird and Freddie Frinton. *Hiawatha* was performed at Scarborough's Pleasure Gardens in 1934.

PIER THEATRE
BOURNEMOUTH

GEORGE & ALFRED BLACK PRESENT

Camp Beds
SOUVENIR PROGRAMME 1/-

HAROLD FIELDING'S

STAR-LIGHT ROOF

at the WINTER GARDENS

PIER PAVILION
GREATREX NEWMAN & HUGH CHARLES
present

The Fol de Rols

Programme 6d.

HIAWATHA
OPEN AIR THEATRE
SCARBOROUGH
1934
SOUVENIR
PROGRAMME
SIXPENCE

▷△ Fol-de-Rols is a long-established phrase associated with theatre, variety and folk music, broadly meaning something trivial and entertaining. It was widely used in pier theatres to describe both the show itself and the performing groups. The summer variety season at Worthing's Pier Pavilion in the 1960s (above) was regularly called the Fol-de-Rols, while George Royle's Fol-de-Rols troupe (right) was performing in the 1930s.

GEORGE ROYLE'S "FOL-DE-ROLS"

▷ Neville Bishop and his Wolves were a well-known seaside theatre group, specializing in the familiar mix of music and comedy, always with plenty of characters of the pantomime dame type – as this 1950s promotional postcard from Great Yarmouth suggests.

▽ Pierrots have been part of theatrical history since the Italian *commedia dell'arte*, and Pierrot groups have been popular seaside performers since the end of the Victorian period. This 1910 card shows a typical group, known as Will Morris's Celebrated Pierrots.

WILL MORRIS'S CELEBRATED PIERROTS 1910.

MERRY FOLK
WESTON-SUPER-MARE, 1922

△ Another promotional card, this time for the Merry Folk, who were appearing at Weston-super-Mare in 1922.

# SEASIDE FUN

In the early days, the sea and the beach were sufficient for visitors, but from the Victorian period seaside resorts began to provide other activities and entertainments. Piers, theatres, bandstands, funfairs and areas for sports and games proliferated, along with shops, cafés and arcades, in many cases encouraged by the uncertainties of the British weather. The traditional appeal of the seaside never waned, but by the end of that era most resorts knew they had to offer more than just sea and sand.

THERE ARE SOME NICE LANDING PLACES FOR SMACKS HERE.

◁ There was a craze for roller skating in the 1930s and another in the 1950s. Many resorts did their best to cater for this, sometimes on a grand scale. The Wellington Pier rink at Great Yarmouth is a good example.

WELLINGTON PIER ROLLER SKATING RINK, GT. YARMOUTH

The Bandstand, Southend-on-Sea

▷ Listening to music was a perennially popular seaside activity, so most resorts had at least one bandstand. This delightful Edwardian example, as ornate as a wedding cake, was at Southend-on-Sea.

◁ Piers were entertainment centres, often offering theatre, concerts and dancing. This 1930s card shows Southampton's Royal Pier, famous at that time for its dance hall.

CONCERTS DANCING

The Royal Pier, Southampton

▷ At Margate the funfair is in full swing and the children's roundabout is spinning round, with lights flashing. For one small boy it is almost too much. Is he shouting with excitement, or does he want to get off?

△ Perched side-saddle on a large carousel horse, this lady seems to be enjoying herself. However, once the carousel begins to turn and the horses rise and fall to the sound of the organ, she will want to hold on to the twisted brass pole rather than her handbag!

# BATHING MACHINES

MARGATE AND SCARBOROUGH both claim the invention of the bathing machine in the 1700s, but these wheeled vehicles designed to protect the modesty of female bathers are particularly associated with the Victorians. Male and female bathing were segregated by law until 1901, after which point the bathing machine gradually disappeared from British beaches.

An unexpected voyage at Blackpool.

▽ Made of wood, or canvas and wood, and mounted on large wheels that raised the cabin 4ft or so, the machines had a ladder and door at each end. These were photographed at Seaford, Sussex, in 1900.

▷ A bathing machine attendant and his horse take a break while a lady is changing into her costume. She will have climbed into a cabin through the 'back' door, and the horse will drag the machine into the sea, where she will enter the water from the 'front' door, well away from male eyes.

△ Posted in 1906, this card illustrates how the machines were used, the costumes that were worn, and the female camaraderie that was all part of the bathing experience.

▷ This Edwardian postcard hints at the new pleasures of mixed bathing following the formal end of segregation. At this point, the privacy of the bathing machine suddenly offered decidedly different prospects.

△ Horses were often used to draw the machines in and out of the sea. However, by the beach pyjama era, the bathing machine was largely extinct.

△ Mixed bathing was legalized in 1901, but this card, sent in 1909 from Bognor Regis, shows bathing machines still in use.

# BEACH HUTS

A LINE OF BRIGHTLY PAINTED wooden beach huts has been a defining feature of the British seaside for about a century. As the bathing machine declined, the beach hut emerged to satisfy the need for a private family space on or near the beach for changing, eating and storage. Like the chalet, beach huts were initially made individually, but gradually the standard factory-made product has taken over. Unlike chalets, many beach huts are available only at certain times of the year and are generally used only in the daytime. Many are privately owned, but more common are rows erected by the local town council and hired out for the season.

△ Against a background of standard beach huts, three girls busy themselves building a sandcastle somewhere in England in 1955.

▽ There are many variations on the basic beach hut. This 1960s card shows the modernist version at Angmering in Sussex, built in terraced blocks with flat roofs and large French windows.

△ The simpler alternative to the beach hut was the changing tent. Here, a line of gaily striped examples forms a backdrop to the three girls posing for the camera.

▽ Classic beach huts, flanking the beach in colourful rows, can be seen in many parts of Britain. This is Sidmouth, in Devon, in the late 1960s.

▷ Making your own beach hut or chalet was always fun, and there were magazines to tell you how to do it. This is a wonderful image of a stereotypical 1950s family happily performing well-defined roles.

△ There's nothing like a good cup of tea. An elderly couple and their dog relax outside their beach hut, savouring the moment.

# DECKCHAIRS

THE ORIGIN OF THE DECKCHAIR is partly explained by its name: it was developed from the folding wooden chairs used at sea. Another source is the camping and campaign furniture used by army officers from the 18th century. However, the seaside deckchair, with its brightly striped canvas and its simple, flat-folding design, is a quite distinct and largely British phenomenon. The standard design, with its propensity for catching the fingers of unwary children, has been part of seaside and garden life for over a century. Variations include versions with foot rests, arm rests and built-in sunshades, double-width chairs for romantic couples, and miniatures for children and dolls. While the deckchair is characteristically striped, those that are hired out on the beach – by the hour or the day – are usually plain, often in municipal green.

▷ Relaxing in deckchairs at Sandown, on the Isle of Wight, in 1948, this couple make a classic period fashion statement. She wears a cardigan, sensible skirt, thick stockings and open shoes, and clasps her handbag on her lap; he is in a cricket jumper, sports jacket with pocket handkerchief and shirt collar neatly overlaid, and white plimsolls.

◁ Serried ranks of municipal deckchairs line the front at some British resort in 1910. It is April, so everyone is well wrapped up but determined to make the most of the sunshine.

◁ This jolly lady is clearly enjoying her holiday in Jersey in the 1950s. Her bedraggled hair and the towel spread over the back of the deckchair suggest she is drying off after a dip in the sea.

▷ It is Swanage beach in 1955, and the caption in the album says it all: ice creams have given Dad a break from sandcastle duties and, perhaps, a few minutes in the deckchair with the newspaper.

◁ In a classic early 1920s image, three friends, or relatives, sit back in their hired deckchairs after a cup of tea. The women look summery in white, with big straw hats, while the man is in a thick tweed suit and heavy walking shoes. At least he wears a boater.

EASTBOURNE CORPORATION Deck Chair 3d Tu5841

Any complaint with reference to collectors should be addressed to Entertainments Manager, Winter Garden, Devonshire Park. It is requested that the ticket be retained and shown to Inspector when called upon. Not transferable. Chairs must NOT be reserved

HAMMICKS

For Confectionery    CARLISLE ROAD

| MORNING | AFTERNOON | EVENING |
| 9 to 2 | 2 to 6 | 6 to 10 |

△ Avoiding the deckchair attendant was a familiar holiday game, but most people had to pay up. This Eastbourne ticket was for the evening session, 6pm to 10pm.

▷ Surprisingly relaxed despite all those clothes, and all those young children, this 1920s family poses happily for the photographer. The mother's deckchair is a superior model, with a fringed sunshade.

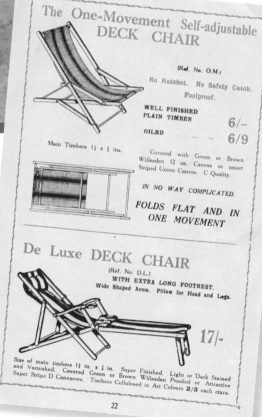

The One-Movement Self-adjustable DECK CHAIR

(Ref. No. O.M.)

No Ratchet.  No Safety Catch.
Foolproof.

WELL FINISHED
PLAIN TIMBER                    6/-
OILED          ...      ...     6/9

Main Timbers 1¼ x ⅞ ins.

Covered with Green or Brown Willesden 12 oz. Canvas or smart Striped Union Canvas. C Quality.

IN NO WAY COMPLICATED.

FOLDS FLAT AND IN ONE MOVEMENT

De Luxe DECK CHAIR

(Ref. No. D.L.)

WITH EXTRA LONG FOOTREST.
Wide Shaped Arms.  Pillow for Head and Legs.

17/-

Size of main timbers 1⅝ in. x ⅞ in.  Super Finished.  Light or Dark Stained and Varnished.  Covered Green or Brown Willesden Proofed or Attractive Super Stripe D Canvasses.  Timbers Cellulosed in Art Colours 2/3 each extra.

22

△ Deckchairs in Yeo Paull of Bristol's 1938 catalogue.

# CHILD'S PLAY

EVERY FAMILY PHOTOGRAPH ALBUM is filled with pictures of children on holiday, playing on the beach or in the playground and casually posing for the camera wielded with greater or lesser skill by mum or dad. The subject matter is unchanging and often predictable, but the period detail can add considerably to the lasting and universal appeal of such images, even when the identities of the children, and their families, have been lost with the passage of time.

◁ It is a windy day in the 1950s on Seaford's stony beach and two girls, most probably sisters, have been carefully posed on a Newhaven-registered fishing boat, drawn up on the shingle.

◁ Four children, wearing ruched and ill-fitting costumes typical of 1957, pose somewhat disconsolately on a pedalo on Saundersfoot beach, in Pembrokeshire. They have probably been told they can sit on it, but hiring it for an outing is not on the agenda that day.

△ A father cheerfully carries the burden of his two little girls, identically dressed and pigtailed, along a sandy beach somewhere in England in the 1950s.

▷ These two are having a lovely time in the park, riding the pitching horse and grinning for the photograph. They are holding on very tightly, as they have no doubt been told to do.

"Never Never Land" your party in the soup

BOOK YOUR HOLIDAY MEALS AT

PETER PAN'S PLAYGROUND

SOUTHPORT

A Sample of some Parties we have Catered for

| | Children | Adults |
|---|---|---|
| BATLEY CARR WORKING MEN'S CLUB | 510 | 46 |
| BRADFORD WARP DYERS | 230 | 18 |
| NEWTOWN BRITISH LEGION | 500 | 100 |
| BARNSLEY TRADES' COUNCIL CLUB | 279 | 50 |
| LUND WOOD CLUB | 700 | 85 |
| HOGHTON VICARAGE | 30 | 30 |

ROUNDABOUTS
MOTOR CARS
AEROPLANES -
NOAHS ARK-SLIDES
JUNGLE RAILWAY
SWINGS - TOYS
ICES - AND A
1001 OTHER JOYS

NO PARTY TOO BIG OR TOO SMALL FOR OUR HIGH CLASS CAFE

The Childrens Paradise

118

◁▽ In a series of high-quality photographs from a now anonymous album, these children were recorded playing in the park and on a beach roundabout on a family holiday in Devon in 1948. The girl at the top of the slide is probably telling her brother: 'Don't you dare follow me!'

▷ In Britain in the early 1950s, beach toys were at a premium, so the old car inner tube was invaluable in teaching the nation's children to swim.

▽ In this classic 1920s seaside image, a dad poses on a makeshift see-saw with his passengers while the old chap on the left, perhaps their grandfather, stands watching. They have probably hired one of the beach huts in the background for the week.

## EVACUEES

When the Blitz started in the summer of 1940, half a million people were evacuated from areas thought likely to be bombed. Most were absorbed into rural villages but some went to remote seaside resorts. City children from close-knit families were moved into an unfamiliar world, miles from their parents, and many suffered desperately from homesickness. Cards like this were produced to cheer them up and persuade them that evacuation was like a holiday.

△ 'I know the water's cold but come on, smile for the camera and look as though you are enjoying yourselves.'

▷ There is plenty to dig for at low tide on Margate beach and this boy doesn't seem to mind that he is wearing his school uniform, even though he is on holiday. The message on the back of the card is, like so many, to the point: 'Train seems to get to Tunbridge Wells Central on Sat. at 6.2. If you are not there will come straight home.'

"Just off for our daily dip!"

△ It is Exmouth in 1937 and Donald, aged five and a half, is very pleased with his new yacht ... but sailing it in the sea is a serious matter.

# DONKEY RIDES

DONKEYS BEGAN TO APPEAR on beaches in the 1780s, but the donkey ride along the sands did not become an essential part of the holiday experience until the Victorian period. By the 1880s donkeys were to be found at most major seaside resorts. In the early days some pulled little carriages or carried children in baskets on their backs, but for the most part the animals – saddled, named and often decorated – were ridden and led at a walking pace in groups. Long, sandy beaches were preferred, with favourites including Blackpool, Skegness, Great Yarmouth, Weymouth and Paignton, and the popularity of donkey riding is reflected in postcards of these and many other resorts. In the past, donkeys worked long hours, often in poor conditions, but legislation has greatly improved their lot, with defined working hours, days off and a weight limit for riders.

▷ Donkeys often feature on humorous cards and puns were always popular. This example was sent from Great Yarmouth in 1906 from a father to his son, at home with his mother. He writes: 'Kiss your mum lots of kisses. It is very cold.'

Yarmouth.

Having a Ripping time.

◁ In this classic holiday snap from the 1950s, the small boy sits, perhaps a little nervously, on a large donkey while his sister, wrapped in her overcoat, looks on.

▽ It is the 1970s in Skegness and the donkeys, as popular as ever, are still hard at work. Names clearly displayed, as in this case, allowed children to pick a favourite.

◁ The donkeys carrying these happy 1920s flappers seem resigned to weights that would nowadays be over the limit.

▽ Posted from St Anne's in 1907, this card shows donkeys ready for duty, some with raised wicker saddles. The sender, writing in French, was amazed that donkeys could be ridden on the beach and that the sea went out beyond the pier!

I simply adore donkeys—when are you coming down?

▽ The message is clear on this 1920s card and the girl's grin shows that she is entirely in agreement.

BETTER THAN SCHOOL.

DONKEY STAND, ST. ANNES-ON-SEA.

▷ Looking to our eyes somewhat overdressed, these Edwardian children await their ride on a pair of shaggy donkeys. The boy, understandably, does not look at ease with his unusual side-saddle position.

# ICE CREAM

VERSIONS OF ICE CREAM may have been made by the Romans, and certainly sorbets were popular in 18th-century Britain, but ice cream as we know it did not appear until the late-Victorian period, along with the cone, by which time new refrigeration techniques had made large-scale production possible. From the mid-1920s a familiar figure at seaside resorts was the 'Stop me and buy one' vendor on his tricycle, first used by Wall's and a forerunner of the modern ice cream van.

"THIS IS MY FOURTEENTH————
I WAS SIMPLY STARVING."

# CREAM GATEAU

## LETTERED ROCK

*Classic rock, a pink-coloured, mint-flavoured, cylindrical pulled-sugar confectionery in the form of a stick, with a text all the way along its centre, first appeared at late-Victorian fairgrounds. It moved to the seaside, probably first to Blackpool and Morecambe, and quickly became the favourite holiday souvenir. Rock's association with cheap holidays, day trips and holiday camps made it hugely popular in the 1950s and 1960s. Rock is made from sugar and glucose, boiled until the mixture can be poured out and rolled into fat cylinders. Flavour and colour are added, and the letters for the message, usually the name of the resort, are moulded individually and inserted into the cylinder, which is then stretched mechanically and rolled by hand until it reaches the right diameter. Finally, it is cut into lengths and wrapped, often with a picture of the resort.*

HAD A SWEET TIME

LYONS ICE CREAM

SMOOTHER

SWEETER

HAVE A WALLSIE GOOD AND BIG!

BUY IT WHERE YOU SEE THE *Wall's* SIGN

SANDWICH COURSE

# SANDCASTLES

▽ This little girl, on holiday in Devon in the late 1940s, is taking her sandcastle duties very seriously and has set up a production line involving two buckets.

GIVE A CHILD a sandy beach, a bucket and a spade and he or she will set to work, building some great construction that might incorporate seaweed, driftwood or other flotsam. It could be a huge mound of sand with a moat or an intricate edifice with towers and pinnacles but, either way, the incoming tide will sweep it away and clear the beach ready for the next day's building programme. Sandcastles have always been a seaside tradition and as a result there have long been sandcastle competitions and even professional sand sculptors.

▷ Taken by an itinerant beach photographer in September 1924, this is Marjorie Platt, and she is not happy. Maybe the impossibility of her task has just struck her, or she does not like being interrupted in the middle of her work.

◁ This is a famous poster issued by the Great Northern Railway in the Edwardian era to promote travel to the East Coast resorts on its network.

▷ Many early postcards exploit the sandcastle theme. This one, sent in 1909 to Mary Knighton, has a suitable message: 'This looks like Morris and you trying to pull Margaret out of the sand – my word, I wish you were here.'

On the Sands at Yarmouth.

A Gallant Rescue

△◁ Sand sculpture has long been a seaside art form, often associated with particular resorts and particular families. The Darrington family has worked on Weymouth beach for generations. Here are two of Fred Darrington's 1970s creations, the Wombles and Tutankhamun.

△ This 1930s Senior Service cigarette card from the 'Holiday Haunts' series shows Filey. 'The beach is excellent for children and the firmness of the sand can easily be judged.'

ENTRENCHED

▽ A sandy beach somewhere in 1950s England and these two pose proudly in the car – or is it a boat? – that they have just completed.

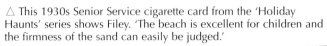

Very Busy.

◁ A delightful Edwardian card of children 'Very Busy' on the beach, this offers an insight into the way children on holiday were dressed in that era.

◁ This card was posted from Lowestoft, in Suffolk, in 1921, from Alice to her friend Nellie in Ipswich, with the message: 'Grand weather. We are nearly scorched out today.'

▷ Despite the caption on the card, this boy did take a break from his classic sandcastle and wrote a quick note from Blackpool to his grandmother back home in Cardiff.

△ This pair, well wrapped up against a cold breeze and ready for the day's sandcastle project, smile for the camera.

# BEACH PARTIES

GROUP PHOTOGRAPHS always offer an entertaining insight into changing attitudes and fashions. Many are from old albums, sadly now separated from the families who took them; others are the work of the professional photographers who frequented resorts through much of the 20th century.

▷ A typical beach photographer working in the 1930s took this jolly group of handsome boys and pretty girls on the sands at Margate, in Kent.

▽ Not quite a fashion parade, more a group of women on a seaside outing, probably in the early 1920s. Hem lines and dress styles vary, from late Edwardian demure to 1920s modern and casual.

△ The quality of this Edwardian image, taken by a professional photographer from Whitby, is remarkable. It is sharp and carefully composed, and everyone looks amazingly well dressed for a stroll along the beach. High collars, hats and watch chains set the standard.

▷ 'Having a Good Time at Hastings!' announces the board in front of this large and varied party, posed in the 1920s by AM Breach, a beach photographer. Too big for a family, and ranging widely in age, the group might have been on a day trip from a nearby town, village or church.

▽ A photograph from a family album, taken perhaps in the late 1920s or the early 1930s. It is a stony beach and, sensibly, everyone is wearing beach shoes. The parasols add an exotic touch.

△ Another Edwardian group, complete with picnic baskets, sticks, an umbrella or parasol and an interesting range of hats, poses in an old boat. And everyone seems to be taking it pretty seriously.

▷ A beach photographer caught this cheerful family in 1923. The photograph was made into a card, which was then sent to a relative in Hong Kong with the message: 'This is us on the beach at Paignton.'

Having a Good Time 228
PHOTO BY A.M.BREACH
AT HASTINGS!

# PUNCH & JUDY

AMONG THE MOST POPULAR and enduring institutions of the British seaside are the saucy postcard and the Punch & Judy show. The latter can trace its origins to 16th-century Italy and the *commedia dell'arte* tradition. Puppet shows featuring the Punch character were being performed in Britain in the 17th century (Samuel Pepys records seeing several). There are many variations on the story, but the stock cast of characters was established by the 1800s: Mr Punch, his wife Judy, their Baby, Joey the Clown, the Dog, the Crocodile, the Policeman – the puppets being operated and spoken by one man, known as the Professor. All ribaldry, violence, social comment and domestic comedy, Punch & Judy is thought to be the origin of slapstick. Still classic seaside entertainment, the show lives on, despite being wonderfully politically incorrect.

▽ Margate was a classic setting for Punch & Judy. Here, in the 1960s, a typical audience – children sitting on the sand at the front, adults in a semi-circle of deckchairs behind – watches the antics of the characters in the standard type of colourful portable theatre. The Professor usually performed several times a day, with the famous Punch line, 'That's the way to do it', a constant refrain.

FORGOTTEN ABOUT SCHOOL
IT'S SO WONDERFUL HERE!

VIVENT LES VACANCES !
L'ECOLE EST OUBLIEE !

▽ Punch & Judy shows, so much a part of the seaside holiday, featured in the publicity brochures produced by many resorts. This example is from the 1950s.

▷ The image of Mr Punch and his family was universally familiar. These drawings of the characters by CH May are taken from a card entitled 'Frolics by the Sea', posted in 1922.

# SEASIDE GAMES

NO SEASIDE HOLIDAY has ever been complete without a game or two, indicative as they are of relaxation and the natural competitive spirit within the family. Most games are informal and are played, frequently with local rules, on the sands, the dunes or the rough grass that often flanks the beach. Generations of children have been introduced to cricket at the seaside. Other popular games include football, kick-the-can and, more recently, frisbee. Equally important are the more formal games, notably bowls and simplified versions of golf, requiring the dedicated playing areas that are to be found in most resorts.

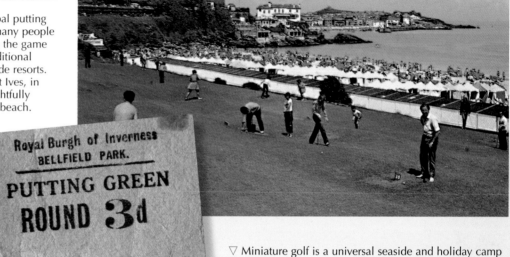

▷ The municipal putting green, where many people first experience the game of golf, is a traditional feature of seaside resorts. This one is at St Ives, in Cornwall, delightfully situated by the beach.

Royal Burgh of Inverness
BELLFIELD PARK.
PUTTING GREEN
ROUND **3d**
11478

▽ Miniature golf is a universal seaside and holiday camp game. This course at Pontin's Camp, Lytham St Anne's, in Lancashire, looks pretty straightforward, but many are more challenging, with fiendishly complicated holes.

▷ This view of the public bowling greens at Fleetwood, in Lancashire, is postmarked 1936. The game has reached a serious moment, but the elegant ladies with their prams have not noticed.

Public Bowling Greens, Marine Gardens, Fleetwood.

3755 Weymouth Corporation Pleasure Gardens.
BOWLS 6d
─. B. Charmbury, Chairman. P.T.O.
Sherrens, Printers, Weymouth.

▽ Against a backdrop of classy beach huts, two suitably jacketed players decide the outcome of a round of bowls at Sandown, on the Isle of Wight, in the 1930s.

▽ Mother looks as if she is ready either to sweep the ball for six or to miss it completely; the other members of the family, clearly expecting the latter, have formed a close field behind the stumps.

△ A classic image of beach cricket at Mablethorpe in the 1920s: the young wicket-keeper, in his school uniform, stands behind the makeshift set of stumps, while his mother faces the bowler with a rather unorthodox stance.

# COMING FOR A DIP?

▽ This 1930s postcard shows Crooklets Beach, Bude, in Cornwall. Most people, one or two in fashionably striped costumes, are just paddling and splashing around, but some daring children are trying out the fairly new beach sport of surf riding. Today, thanks to its great Atlantic rollers, Bude is an international surfing centre.

IT WAS IN THE 18TH CENTURY that sea bathing first became fashionable, for reasons of health, and it was not until the Victorian era that the seaside was seen as fun. For a while the fun was limited by constraints such as bathing machines, all-embracing costumes and strict segregation of the sexes, but by the late 1800s the sea had become the free-for-all it is today. Generations of family snaps and holiday postcards have celebrated this passion for playing in the sea.

SURF RIDING, CROOKLETS BEACH, BUDE.

23874 Sea Urchins.

△ This hand-coloured 1910 postcard, entitled 'Sea Urchins', shows a group of paddling children. Trousers have been hitched up above the knee and long summer dresses have been stuffed into big stripey bloomers.

▷ These handsome lads cheerfully show off their towels (and much else besides) on a sandy beach somewhere in Britain, probably in the 1930s.

**SEASIDE FROLICS.**

▽ A large family or group of friends has been caught by the beach photographer. You can hear the shouts: 'Come on in, the water's lovely!' The costumes, the hair styles and the number of rubber bathing hats suggest it is the 1930s.

▷ This 1950s family-album snap delightfully captures the excitement that the seaside holds for children. No doubt the four friends pictured here are about to plunge into the water, totally unconcerned about its temperature.

**"You can't fool us Auntie—you're holding the BEACH BALL behind your back!"**

# BOAT TRIPS

No seaside holiday was ever complete without a boat trip or two, and most resorts offered plenty of options. There were trips around the bay or to the lighthouse, frequently operated by local fishermen in a variety of craft. Then there were scheduled services on larger vessels, aimed at both the regular traveller and the day tripper. A third option was the charter trade, often catering for group outings on classic vessels.

DAY EXCURSIONS
By sea
FROM WEYMOUTH

CHANNEL ISLANDS
Guernsey and Jersey

FRANCE Cherbourg
No Passport

SOUTHERN
BRITISH RAILWAYS

1962

UNTIL SEPTEMBER 13th, 1959
THE TWIN-SCREW M.V.
"ROYAL SOVEREIGN"

will leave SOUTHEND PIERHEAD DAILY (Fridays excepted)
at 12.0 noon — No Sailing on SUNDAY, 21st JUNE
for 4 HOURS SEA CRUISE and 2 HOURS ASHORE at

MARGATE

The popular Holiday Resort on the Kent coast
Arriving at 2.0 p.m. Leaving 4.0 p.m. Back at SOUTHEND 8.0 p.m.

FARES:    SINGLE    DAY RETURN    PERIOD RETURN
          10/-      13/-          17/6
CHILDREN: Under 3 years FREE    3 to 14 years HALF FARE

Fully Licensed Meals and Light Refreshments Aboard

Sailings are subject to weather and other circumstances permitting

TICKETS INCLUDE ADMISSION TO PIERS

EAGLE & QUEEN LINE STEAMERS
... HILL, SOUTHEND-ON-SEA. Telephone: 66587 (May/Sept)
P.T.O

△ Scheduled services were well advertised, and in the late 1950s and early 1960s the Eagle Line's ships, such as the *Royal Sovereign*, were a familiar sight on the Thames tideway, linking Southend, Clacton, Margate and Ramsgate. In the same period, British Railways operated a large steamer fleet, offering many day trips, including Weymouth to the Channel Islands and Cherbourg.

◁ Eager anticipation shows in the faces of this diverse group at the start of a day trip from an East Coast port in the 1920s.

R.M.V. SCILLONIAN LEAVING SCILLY.

△ Many ships operating between Penzance and the Scilly Islands have been called the *Scillonian*. This example was probably in service in the late 1950s.

▷ By the 1950s the heyday of the Thames sailing barge was over, and a number of these classic vessels went into the charter business. Typical was the *Arrow*, built in Rochester in 1897 and available for charter in 1952. These friends are clearly enjoying a sailing barge experience at about that time.

FOR CHARTER
156-TON SAILING BARGE 'ARROW'

FOR MID WEEK OR
WEEKEND CRUISING
ON THAMES
OR MEDWAY

Applications to: HON. SECRETARY T.B.S.C.
26 CROOMS HILL, S.E. 10.

"There gangs anither shillin's worth."

△ Edwardian day trippers pose for the camera while awaiting departure from Ramsgate. The crew will have a struggle to sail such a densely packed vessel – Health and Safety would have something to say nowadays!

BOROUGH OF TORQUAY
TOLL OR
LANDING AND
EMBARKING
2ᴰ
HALDON PIER
B16840

▽ Local trip boats were always interestingly diverse. This 1950s publicity photograph shows, on the right, a traditional open-decked, clinker-built vessel. In the foreground an amphibious ex-army Dukw (or Duck) sets off across the beach and into the water. These American vehicles, built by General Motors, were frequent visitors to British beaches at this time.

# PADDLE STEAMERS

FROM THE LATE-VICTORIAN PERIOD one of the most common vessels to be seen around the coast of Britain was the paddle steamer. Hundreds of these popular and highly manoeuvrable vessels were built, many in the shipyards of Scotland, for passenger services in coastal waters and river estuaries. They could operate from busy harbours, remote quays and sandy beaches, and until the 1960s no holiday was complete without a trip on a paddle steamer.

▽ The Clyde was home to many famous paddle steamers. A popular trip was the run from Glasgow down to Rothesay, on the Isle of Bute. This gloriously evocative, hand-tinted Edwardian photograph shows the harbour at Rothesay's West Bay: at nearly 4.30pm, crowds gather on the quay for the return trip up the Clyde on the two steamers that await them.

▽ The sound of splashing paddle wheels was so much part and parcel of many seaside resorts that paddle steamers were often shown on multiview cards. This 1920s example was published in Yarmouth, Isle of Wight, the destination for services from Lymington, on the mainland.

▽ The *Medway Queen* was a famous and long-lived paddle steamer, operating along the tidal Thames and around the Thames and Medway estuaries. This card was sent from Clacton in 1951, with the message: 'Had a grand trip & weather is perfect.'

P.S. MEDWAY QUEEN.

△ Written on the back of this photograph is: 'Mum and Dad on a steamer, 1924.' Presumably they are the couple on the left, but everyone is smiling for the camera – except for the lad with his tray of confectionery. For him, it is just another day, just another trip.

◁ Paddle steamers often moved around the coast of Britain as one operator sold them on to another. These moves became more frequent as the steamers aged, and the *Isle of Arran* was quite old when she came to London in 1933 to operate trips around the London docks and along the busy Thames.

ISLE OF ARRAN

P.S. CONSUL IN LULWORTH COVE

△ Paddle steamers could, and frequently did, operate from popular beaches, with gangplanks set out from the bow. This 1920s postcard shows the PS *Consul*, one of a number of familiar visitors to Dorset's Lulworth Cove.

▷ In August 1924 the decks of the PS *Bournemouth Queen* are packed with well-dressed passengers enjoying the sun, and the photographer's antics, as they wait for the lines to be cast off.

# SEASIDE GIRLS

POSTCARDS AND PRETTY GIRLS on the beach have been inseparable since the early 1900s. The result is thousands of postcard images of bathing beauties, drawn and photographed, that are fun, alluring and discreetly – or even overtly – erotic. Not many seem to have been posted, suggesting that most were bought to be kept. As a whole, they offer an entertaining guide to changing beach fashions and to the many ways in which the female body has been posed and presented over the years.

▷ This decorative, full-frontal card was sent by Ann in the 1960s with an equally full-frontal message: 'This is in case you have forgotten what I look like!! Longing to get you here.'

◁ The appeal of the pretty girl was universal in the postcard world. In this example, gently hand coloured, the girl is showing off her summer straw hat. It was sent as a birthday card in 1914.

## I'LL BE LOOKING OUT FOR YOU!

◁▽ The double entendre, the innuendo and the saucy drawing have always been part of the seaside postcard story. Two examples here come from very different eras, the Edwardian (below) and the 1950s, yet, surprisingly, it is the Edwardian one that is the more suggestive. Neither card was written or posted.

IT MAY BE HOT ON TOP OF THE CLIFFS, BUT IT'S VERY COOL HERE AT THE BOTTOM.

◁▷ ▽ Four cards, two Edwardian (left, top and bottom), one 1920s (right) and one 1950s (below), show how bathing belles and their costumes changed over that time. Also revealing is the shift in style, from colour drawing to beach-location photograph, with posed studio portrait in between.

Is he coming this way?

# A WEEK ON THE NORFOLK BROADS – MAY 1936

1. Our worthy craft, the ML *Eddy Wind Two*, moored at Waxham, on the New Cut.

2. Time for tea and biscuits in the cabin.

3. A view of the galley and washing facilities – all mod cons! We were now moored at West Somerton.

④

⑥

⑤

⑦

4. A BIT OF A BLOW IN THE DINGHY AT WEST SOMERTON.

5. MANPOWER WAS NEEDED TO HELP US ALONG THE NEW CUT.

6. OUR MOORING FOR THE NIGHT AT BECCLES — IT WAS A LONG WAY FROM THE PUB!

7. WE MADE IT! JOURNEY'S END AT YARMOUTH AND A RATHER HIGH TIDE.

# CROMER

AS A RESORT, Cromer dates back to the late 18th century, but the town has a much older history as a port and fishing harbour. The church, with its grand tower – the tallest in Norfolk, reflects the region's great medieval wealth. Another legacy is the reputation for crab fishing, with Cromer crabs still widely regarded as a delicacy. The lifeboat has also put Cromer firmly on the map. Henry Blogg, one of the world's greatest lifeboatmen, was coxswain from 1909 to 1947 and is commemorated in the lifeboat museum.

CROMER

*Gem of the Norfolk Coast*

R.H.

146

▲ A typical multiview card, this was posted by a holidaymaker in 1949.

◄ This copy of the official guidebook dates from the 1960s.

► A 1930s aerial view shows the grand church, the strong sea wall and the beaches.

7280                    AERIAL

West Cliff and Beach, Cromer

NOTES & ILLUSTRATIONS
IN COLOUR AND LINE
BY C. A. HANNAFORD R.B.A.

▲▶ Cromer is flanked by cliffs and long, sandy beaches to the west and the east, as seen on these two Edwardian cards.

East Cliff and Beach, Cromer

*The Charm of the*
NORFOLK BROADS

▲ Many visitors have used Cromer as a base for explorations of the Norfolk Broads.

◀ Cromer's famous lifeboat is launched from a slipway at the end of the pier.

PAN-AERO PICTURES
KINGSTON-ON-THAMES

LAUNCHING THE MOTOR LIFEBOAT AT CROMER.

Photo. H. H. Tansley, Cromer

A Magazine of the Footpath and the Open Road

VOL. 1. No. 1.

EDITED BY JOHN E. WALSH

# *The* TRAMPER & CYCLIST

## 3D MONTHLY

### MARCH

When runnels began to
  leap and sing
And daffodil sheaths to
  blow,
Then out of the thicket
  came blue-eyed Spring
And laughed at the melt-
  ing snow.
"It is time, old Winter,
  you went," she said,
And flitted across the
  plain,
With an iris scarf around
  her head
And diamonded with rain.

ALFRED AUSTIN.

1934

# THE GREAT OUTDOORS

"*After a day's walk everything has twice its usual value.*"

GEORGE MACAULAY TREVELYAN (1876–1962)

# HILLS & DALES

IT WAS NOT UNTIL the end of the Victorian era that walking, rambling and rock climbing became popular pastimes. Much of Britain's landscape was still inaccessible, so the walking and climbing were often organized by clubs and groups such as the Ramblers Association and the Youth Hostels Association. Favourite areas were Wales, Scotland, the Lake District and the Derbyshire Dales. From the 1930s walking and climbing became much more popular, encouraged by a proliferation of guidebooks.

▽ A jolly walking group poses outside a hostel in the Lake District in the 1950s. It must be the beginning of the day as everyone looks cheerful and relaxed, and clothes and shoes are clean. By the end of what promises to be a hard day, it will be a different picture.

▽ The YHA was set up in the early 1900s to provide simple accommodation for ramblers, cyclists and youth organizations. Today there are over 200 hostels across Britain, some very remote. This card, written in 1961, shows Copper Mines, in the Lake District. The writer commented on the isolation ('11/5 miles from anywhere'), the primitiveness ('no electricity, hot water to be fetched'), the piano in the common room, the excellent atmosphere and the 'comfy beds'.

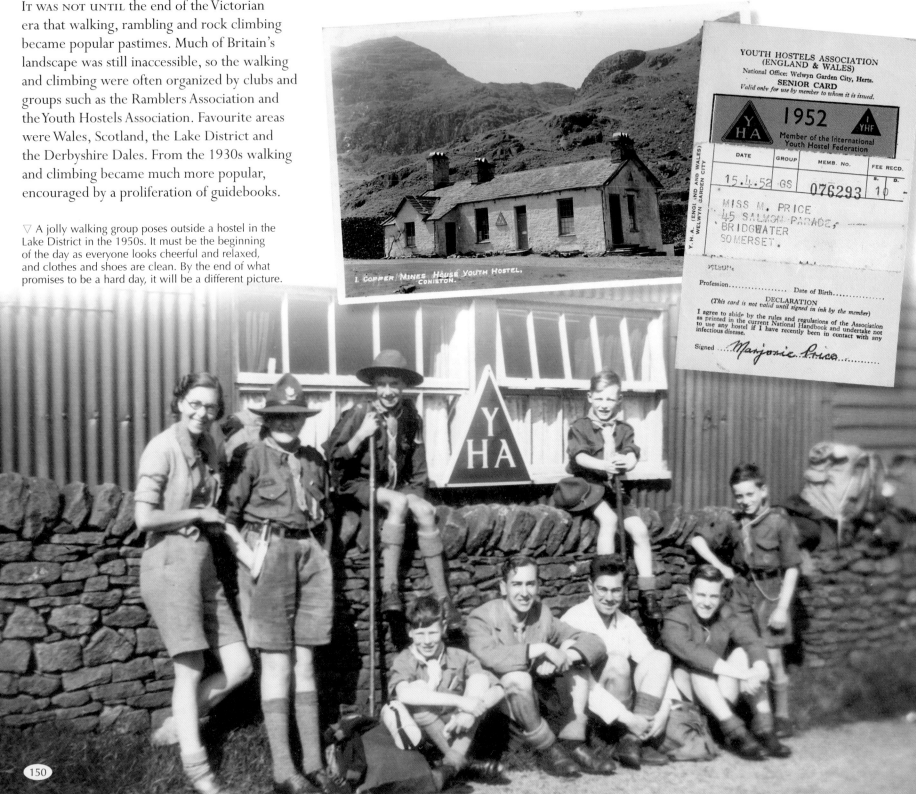

◁ All walkers need a good stick, and this proud gentleman has some excellent ones on show at a country fair or similar event in the 1920s.

▷ This chap looks pleased with the way the climb has gone, but the friend who took the photograph wrote on the back: 'At the top. I was afraid his trousers would fall off.'

Rock climbing in the English Lakes.

Having a high old time.

A.2294

**CONDUCTED RAMBLE**

THE THAMES VALLEY

SUNDAY 16th OCTOBER 1955

BRITISH RAILWAYS
WESTERN REGION

**WALKING**
AT WEEK-ENDS
BY
S. P. B. MAIS

Published by the
Southern Railway

PRICE SIXPENCE

◁ Railway and bus companies began to encourage walking in the 1930s, running excursions and issuing guidebooks. SPB Mais wrote several walking guides for the Southern Railway in the 1930s. British Railways continued the tradition from the 1940s, promoting walks led by the Ramblers Association on routes that linked two stations. The return fare for the Thames Valley conducted ramble in 1955 was 5s 0d (25p).

▷ Time for a welcome breather surrounded by magnificent scenery, perhaps in Scotland.

# CYCLING

THE MODERN SAFETY BICYCLE was developed in the 1870s and from that moment cycling took the nation by storm. The new freedom offered by the bicycle was enjoyed by thousands, and cycling clubs were soon established all over the country, attracting both men and women who, for the first time, were able to explore and enjoy their own countryside. The bicycle became the favourite holiday vehicle.

▽ There were many variations on the standard bicycle. Here Edwardian twins, identically dressed, down to their bracelets, pose for the camera before setting off for a holiday ride. The wicker trailer looks fun for the passenger, but it must have been very hard work for the bicyclist on her upright ladies' machine.

"WHAT ABOUT CHANGING PLACES, GEORGE? THE VIEW FROM HERE IS GETTING RATHER MONOTONOUS."

▽ Another variant was this kind of quadricycle, a two- or three-seater vehicle often to be found at seaside resorts and holiday camps. This particular model was photographed in the 1960s at the Trecco Bay Holiday Camp, near Porthcawl, in Wales. In the background a child rides past the parked Mini on another strange-looking bicycle. The inset photograph shows an older, and slightly more sporty, quadricycle in use at a camp on the Isle of Wight in the 1950s.

△ The full impact of the bicycle on Edwardian Britain can be seen in this group setting off on a country ride. All are wearing fashionable, and suitable, clothing: plus fours for the men and the correct kind of skirt for the lady. Her bicycle has the latest, fully enclosed chain.

▽▷ Maps for cycle touring were readily available from the 1900s. Bartholomew began issuing theirs in the Edwardian era, Geographia in the 1930s. There were famous bicycle-makers too, mostly in the Midlands. The 1956 BSA catalogue has a full range of touring and sports machines for men, women and children, along with special shopping and keep-fit models.

PRICE ONE SHILLING

BARTHOLOMEW'S
REDUCED
ORDNANCE SURVEY

SHEET 36.
SOUTH DEVON
Scale 2 Miles to an Inch.
COLOURED
FOR
TOURISTS & CYCLISTS

JOHN BARTHOLOMEW & CO.
Edinburgh Geographical Institute
PARK ROAD ✢ EDINBURGH

"GEOGRAPHIA"
Cyclists' Map
No. 1
SOUTH EAST COUNTIES

Showing Arterial, First Class, and other Roads.

9

Published by
"GEOGRAPHIA" LTD
167 Fleet Street, London. E.C.4.

△ Some keen cyclist and home movie enthusiast constructed this in Surrey, probably in the 1950s. An 8mm film camera mounted on a gent's tourer could give a whole new definition to the phrase 'moving pictures' – and really bring those holiday snaps to life.

by cycle

cycle by BSA

◁ Phyl and Henry sent this card to Mum and Dad while on holiday in Hove in the 1930s. Henry, for one, is clearly a serious cyclist, sporting cycling shoes, long socks, bare knees, shorts and a tie. Like so many of his contemporaries, he is a cigarette-smoker.

▷ The Nottingham-based Raleigh company was another famous name, and the sporting quality of their bicycles was underlined by the images in the 1929 catalogue.

▽ These keen 1950s students are on an outing into the country. Most have a bicycle basket, probably carrying refreshments, and some of the girls seem to have picked wild flowers.

# HOLE IN ONE!

GOLF, IN ONE FORM OR ANOTHER, has been played in Britain for centuries, but the game as we know it today first became popular during the late-Victorian period. From that time, and especially in the 1920s, numerous new golf clubs and courses, both private and public, opened, becoming important features of many seaside and holiday resorts. Amateur players were also encouraged by dedicated golfing holidays and hotels, which offered them entertainment as well as a chance to improve their game.

**Powfoot Golf Hotel**

ON THE SHORES OF THE SOLWAY FIRTH

Telegrams:
HOTEL CUMMERTREES
Telephone:
254 CUMMERTREES

Golf free
to Hotel
Residents

▽ The pitch and putt course was for many people an easy introduction to the game. Here, at a seaside resort in the 1950s, a family gets to grips with the challenges of some rather rough and rudimentary greens.

△ Scotland has long been renowned for its golf courses, so generations of players, professional and amateur, have been drawn north of the border, often to stay in specialist golf hotels. This brochure from the Powfoot Golf Hotel in Cummertrees, Dumfriesshire, offered residents full board at 14 guineas (£14.70) per week and no green fees.

◁ A round of golf might offer ample opportunities for flirting and romance. In this 1928 photograph, he looks ready to get on with the game, but she perhaps has other things on her mind.

11919

"Oh, Mr. Mustard. Would you like to play a round with me?"

▷▽ By the 1920s women had begun to take up golf in significant numbers. These two show differing attitudes: one seems to be taking the game seriously, although by today's standards she has only a small selection of clubs in her bag, while the other seems rather more frivolous.

◁ A 1920s couple have adopted very competitive poses for this photograph outside the club house. However, the way they hold their putters suggests a certain lack of dedication to the game.

# ANYONE FOR TENNIS?

THE MODERN GAME OF LAWN TENNIS was developed in the 1860s. Initially aimed at families, and marketed as a suitable game for women and children and as a game that men and women could play together, it soon became a seriously competitive sport. The first Wimbledon Tournament was held in 1877, and by the Edwardian era tennis had achieved widespread popularity, with clubs across the world. By the 1920s the social aspects had become as important as the sport itself, a theme in John Betjeman's poems. Soon tennis courts were to be found in public parks, by the sea, at hotels and in holiday camps.

▽ From the early 1900s there was a demand for dedicated sports clothing, and many manufacturers and retailers began to concentrate on this important market. This 1929 North British catalogue features shoes for tennis, bowls, running, bathing and boating.

▷ This 1920s hand-tinted photograph shows a pretty girl posed by the beach. It is not clear whether she is on her way to the courts or whether her racquet is just a fashion accessory.

**NORTH BRITISH**

SPORTS SHOES & BATHING SANDALS

for the Summer of 1929

Chamberlins Ltd.
5 Market Place
NORWICH

▷ By the 1940s and 1950s many holiday camps had tennis courts. This card, posted in 1948, shows the courts and a fine range of chalets at Seacroft Camp in North Norfolk, with a mixed doubles match under way.

◁ Early postcards often hinted at the importance of the social, and romantic, aspects of tennis. This example, postmarked 1913, shows a typical courting couple. They are dressed for tennis and she is still clinging to her racquet, but they have certainly taken their eyes off the ball.

M. E. LTD.
TENNIS
4 PLAYERS 2/8
FROM | TO | COURT

TENNIS COURTS

◁ Judging by their immaculate outfits and generally *soigné* look, these 1930s aficionados are ready for a game or two. Someone will have to sit and watch, and it is unlikely to be the girl!

▷ This Edwardian card suggests that tennis could be just an excuse for all kinds of other activities. It was posted in 1910, with the message: 'My dear Lucy, Thanks for your ripping letter. I roared over it. It won't be long before I see you again.'

When tired of Tennis, try Spooning!

◁ Pigtails, tennis dresses, white flannel trousers and generally tousled hairdos indicate that these players have been hard at work on the courts in Perranporth, Cornwall, in 1933.

SEACROFT HOLIDAY CAMP. HEMSBY-ON-SEA. NORFOLK

△ A cheerful family poses before the game. The clothing is a bit ad hoc, but the young chap on the right, casually resting on the net, will be taking things seriously.

# MESSING ABOUT

THE PLEASURES, AND THE THRILLS, of getting out on the water in a yacht or a rowing boat have been appreciated for decades. Adventure stories have often been the inspiration for the generations of children who have been sent out to test their skills – but all too frequently the learning curve has been a rapid one, as lively imagination has had to come to terms with the hard reality of crewing a small boat on a cold, wet and windy day.

△ It is the 1930s and four Girl Guides pose on an old fishing boat, acting out some great adventure. The reality is that it is low tide, the boat is firmly aground and, with no sails rigged, they won't be going anywhere.

△ 'Yachting, A Stiff Breeze' is the title of this 1920s card showing a large racing yacht making the most of the wind, perhaps in the Solent. The wind must be fluky, as the yacht in the background is barely moving.

▽ Classic children's sailing, represented by a GP14 on a family holiday in 1958.

△ The caption says: 'Paul and John and self, taken by Sylvia on Hickling Broad.' The Norfolk Broads, not demanding great experience, has been popular for sailing and other boating holidays since the late 1800s.

▽ Summer frocks, a breeze in the hair and the sail, a firm hand on the tiller and a patient dog – *The Famous Five* or *Swallows and Amazons*?

▽ In a scene familiar in harbours and sailing clubs all over Britain, racing yachts are readied for action. This is Lowestoft in the 1960s, but the writer of this card wasn't doing much sailing: 'Spend most of the time swimming and eating. Must have put on pounds.'

▷ Clustered in the bow of an old clinker-built fishing boat off the coast of Cornwall, this happy group is enjoying a trip round the bay. One of the men has a Leica slung round his neck, so there must have been two photographers in the party.

YACHT BASIN & R.N.&S.Y. CLUB, LOWESTOFT

Ford Jenkins

▷ Though very popular today, the twin-hulled catamaran was a rare sight in Britain until the 1950s. This 1960s card shows an early example, *Endeavour*, at speed in the Solent.

△ Sailing a boat straight onto the hard stones of Brighton beach would be risky at the best of times, but this chap has obviously managed to do it. The Palace Pier is in the background.

△ With oars casually abandoned, these three young people, dressed in a variety of 1930s styles, have seen something to make them ignore all conventional boating rules and stand up. Let's hope it didn't end in disaster.

▷ The waves are rolling onto the beach at Skegness in 1914 as six pretty girls, elegantly dressed as always in that era, wait for their rowing boat to be launched. The small boy in a striking blazer, with his shoes hung from his belt, may be helping. The message, from Maud to Lydia, in London, says: 'Do you know anyone here?'

# HOLIDAY AFLOAT

CHARLES DICKENS wrote a guide to the river Thames, and he was by no means the first writer to extol the pleasures of waterways. The British have long enjoyed spending time in boats on rivers, canals and lakes, whether on day trips or organized holidays, and the pleasures that inland waterways offer seem to be universal in their appeal.

▽ The canal network dates back to the 18th century, but canal cruising for pleasure is a relatively recent development. In a classic conjunction of canal, bridge, boat and pub, this 1970s card shows a modern steel hire cruiser at Talybont, on the Brecon-to-Abergavenny canal in Wales.

▷ This card, postmarked 1909, shows a crowded Boulter's Lock near Maidenhead, on the Thames. At that time, a trip to this stretch of the river was the ultimate fashionable outing for Londoners. On a sunny weekend simply everyone who was anyone descended on the river, and those who couldn't get into boats stood and watched.

◁▷ The Norfolk Broads was one of Britain's first inland waterway regions to be developed for pleasure boating. Hire cruisers were available there well before World War II, as indicated by the photograph on the left. This shows a 1930s family posing on a typical old-style, wooden Broads cruiser. Since then, the appeal of a 'Holiday Afloat' on the Broads has increased hugely, encouraged by a number of well-known names in the hire boat industry, including Blakes.

▽ This large and wonderfully diverse group, enjoying an outing on the Thames launch *Windsor Castle*, was photographed in a lock somewhere on the river in the 1930s.

◁ For those who want to enjoy the pleasures of the river without moving, a houseboat was the ideal option. An Edwardian party has gathered for a photograph on this elegant craft, moored somewhere on the Thames. And when lazing in the wicker chairs begins to pall, there is always be a trip in the skiff or the canoe.

◁ Anyone who has read *Three Men in a Boat* will know all about the pleasures, and the pitfalls, of the camping skiff. This chap seems to be coping well as he enjoys his tea, laid out on a well-laundered tablecloth. However, hat, coat and suitcase perhaps indicate that he has only recently arrived and reality has yet to set in.

△ The card suggests a glorious day on the Oxford Canal in 1971, but the truth lies in the message on the back: 'Rained all day. Boat stopped with blanket round the prop. Bounced off a few locks, but am still smiling.'

▽ It is wartime, but there is still time for a short break on the river. This gentleman is making the most of his escape from harsh reality in 1942 as he steers the wooden *Carina* along a stretch of the Thames.

British Waterways 'Heart of England' Cruises 1960

between Oxford and Birmingham in m.v. 'WATER RAMBLER'

△ Waterways literature ranges from the pioneering book *Our Holiday on a Barge*, published in 1911, to little 1950s and 1960s guides to some of Britain's lesser-known rivers.

▷ (Inset) British Waterways did much to promote pleasure boating. Their cruiser *Water Rambler* operated services between Oxford and Birmingham, with overnight stays in hotels.

# WHAT A CATCH!

FISHING HAS ALWAYS BEEN a serious business, and the dedicated fisherman will stop at nothing to ensure the quality of his day's sport. At the same time, it is a very accessible activity and something that can be fitted into holidays of many types, at any level and to suit all ages and all pockets. For children, catching tiddlers in a stream or in a rock pool on the beach is endlessly absorbing and can be the start of a lifelong obsession.

▷ It is 1949 in Devon and in a classic holiday image, grandpa has taken the children down to the rocks to teach them the rudiments of sea fishing.

△ Judging by her gear and the size of the salmon she is holding, this lady has had plenty of fly-fishing practice. All those hours of patiently waiting for a bite and teasing the fish have paid off.

▷ These chaps, perhaps part of an Edwardian house party on a large Scottish estate, have had a good day on the river, or the loch, catching trout and other fish. They don't need to worry about the ones that got away.

◁ The lady members of the same Edwardian house party have not done quite so well. To a modern eye, the large hats and long skirts hardly look like suitable fishing wear.

▽ On a trout stream somewhere in 1920s England two men pose for the camera, their fly rods ready in their hands. Today, their clothing might raise a few eyebrows in serious game-fishing circles.

26 AUG

S.E. Stock (2220)

SOUTHERN RAILWAY COMPANY.

FOLKESTONE PIER

DAY FISHING TICKET.

NOT TRANSFERABLE.

No. 59566          Price 6d.

[OVER.

# FAMILY & FRIENDS

SINCE THE 1900s the availability of portable, simply operated, roll-film cameras has made photography a national pastime. All aspects of life have been captured by generations of amateurs. Many images are personal, but notable – particularly in albums – are the numerous photographs of people having a good time together on holiday.

▷ Sometime in the 1930s a photographer has captured a glorious moment as smart grown-ups let their hair down on a children's see-saw. The boy in the centre struggles to restore the balance.

▽ It is impossible to imagine what brought these people together on top of a cliff on a sunny day. They vary in age and dress style, but are too numerous to belong to one family.

▷ This redoubtable 1930s group, probably one family, is out walking in the hills. Sensible clothes, with plenty of tweeds, seem to be the order of the day.

▷ Two elegant ladies, possibly sisters, have seized the moment for a rest beneath a tree. They wear badges, so they are probably on an organized outing to the country, perhaps with the WI.

▽ A 1930s coach party, complete with driver, gathers for a formal group photograph to commemorate a visit to the Cheddar Gorge.

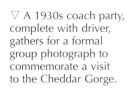

VISITING GOUGH'S CAVES CHEDDAR

◁ The members of this huge group smile for the photographer in a flowery field somewhere in Edwardian Britain. Most are wearing hats, wide-brimmed ones for the ladies, caps for the men. Meanwhile, on the road at the top, a passer-by is watching it all, no doubt with some amazement.

△ These friends, all wearing berets, sit close together, probably on the instructions of the itinerant photographer, to mark their visit to the Giant's Causeway in Northern Ireland, sometime in the 1930s.

# HAVING A PICNIC

MEALS HAVE BEEN EATEN out of doors in Britain for centuries, but the concept of the picnic as enjoyed today, and the word itself, seem to date from the late 17th century. The origins are probably French: *piquer*, to peck, and *nique*, nothing. In the Victorian and Edwardian eras the picnic could be quite a grand affair, but it became more informal in the 20th century, helped by the popularity of camping and the wider use of bicycles, cars and motor buses. In turn, all this encouraged the development of such dedicated picnic equipment as folding chairs, portable kettles and the fully fitted picnic basket.

△ This card was produced in about 1961 to promote the Austin Seven Countryman, one of the range of small cars later known collectively as Minis. This iconic vehicle, with its convertible back seats and barn-style rear doors, was perfect for a day at the seaside with the dog and, of course, a picnic.

◁ Mother and daughter have made themselves comfortable on the seats they have taken out of the car and are enjoying a cup of tea from the Thermos flasks in the basket.

△ An elderly couple have gone out for a spin and have parked by the beach. He has taken the folding chairs and the picnic basket out of the boot, along with a bottle of milk, and poses while she takes the picture.

△ This picnic outing is a magnificent vision of Edwardian England. Most members of the group are hatted, the women extravagantly so. Two ladies rest in the Landau, while the horses graze out of view. The scattered crockery on the grass suggests the picnic has already been eaten.

△ Just the right spot has been chosen for a picnic beside the party's two cars, an old Riley and a newish Ford Popular. While the grown-ups struggle with the folding chairs, a cheerful-looking teenager and a younger boy in cap and sunglasses pose for the camera. Beside them is that 1950s novelty, the Vidor portable radio, tuned, no doubt, to the Light Programme.

◁ It is Horsey Beach in Norfolk in 1934. The sea is calm, the sun is shining, a rug has been spread out on the dunes and everyone looks relaxed and cheerful: the perfect picnic.

## PICNIC EQUIPMENT

*The picnic basket or hamper is as old as the habit of eating out of doors. Initially, food and utensils were carried in ordinary baskets and boxes, but the fitted wicker hamper became popular in the Victorian era. By the end of the 19th century there was a vast choice of hampers, along with related equipment such as the picnic kettle, available for all levels of the market, notably from retailers such as the Army & Navy Stores. In the 20th century, metals and plastics were used for boxes and fittings, often in fashionable styles, but traditional wicker has made a comeback in recent decades.*

SIRRAM PICNIC KETTLE

No. 102 .. 2¼ pint

A sectional view of the set in use

Made in England by Marris's Ltd., Cumberland St., Birmingham, I

# OUR MOTOR TOUR IN ENGLAND – 1933

**②**

**①**

**③**

1. A ROADSIDE HALT BETWEEN DAWLISH AND TEIGNMOUTH, IN DEVON – JUST THE TWO OF US.

2. THE FAMILY CAMP IN A FIELD NEAR STARCROSS, IN DEVON – A CHANCE TO CATCH UP WITH THE WASHING!

3. THE FAITHFUL FORD AT REST NEAR EASTBOURNE, IN SUSSEX, WHILE WE ENJOYED THE WONDERFUL VIEW. NOT MUCH TRAFFIC, BUT A BIT MISTY.

④

⑥

⑤

⑦

4. ON THE BRIGHTON ROAD WITH TOM.

5. AFTER LUNCHING WITH THE GREGORYS IN THEIR NEW HOUSE NEAR NEWHAVEN, SUSSEX.

6. HERE WE ARE IN FRINTON, IN ESSEX – RATHER A QUIET LITTLE PLACE.

7. WE ARRIVE IN OXFORD. WE ARE OUTSIDE MAGDALEN COLLEGE.

# BLACKPOOL

IN MANY WAYS BLACKPOOL is the classic British seaside resort. Its origins go back to the early 19th century, but its development was essentially Victorian, linked closely to the wakes week holidays of the Lancashire mills. The railway came in 1846, and by the 1890s visitor numbers had swelled to 250,000. The Golden Mile, with its long beach, three piers and pioneering electric tramway, set the scene, while the Winter Gardens and the Tower ensured Blackpool was synonymous with holiday fun. By 1930 it was catering for seven million visitors every year.

MAXIM FLYING MACHINE, BLACKPOOL, TRAVELLING 40 MILES AN HOUR.

◀ In the Edwardian era the fairground rides were just the biggest and the best.

▲ The Illuminations as we know them started in 1912, to commemorate the first visit to Blackpool by a member of the royal family.

▶ The ballroom was just one of the entertainment venues in the Tower complex.

TOWER BALLROOM, BLACKPOOL.

▲ Running from the end of August for 60 days until early November, the Illuminations stretch for 6 miles and use more than a million light bulbs.

I CAN'T BEAR THE THOUGHT OF GOING BACK TO SCHOOL NEXT WEEK AND LEAVING BLACKPOOL.

▲ This scene was captured in 1948, when Blackpool was still one of Britain's favourite holiday destinations.

▶ The Tower, opened in 1894, really put Blackpool on the map.

LANCASHIRE COAST & WIRRAL PENINSULA (CHESHIRE)

LANDMARK OF BLACKPOOL'S ENTERTAINMENT AND SHOWPLACES

Famed the world over as the mecca of Britain's holidaymakers

TOWER

with its

* Unrivalled Circus
* Magnificent Ballroom
* Menagerie
* Aquarium
* Roof Gardens
* Ascent
* Restaurant and Cafés

Dancing to
FREDDIE PLATT
and the Tower Band

REGINALD DIXON
at the Organ

TOWER OPEN ALL THE YEAR ROUND

General Admission - 1/9 inc. tax

When replying to Advertisers please mention this Guide.

ILLUMINATIONS

EVENING TRIP
TO

BLACKPOOL

WEDNESDAY 21st SEPTEMBER 1955

| FROM | TIMES OF DEPARTURE | RETURN FARES Third Class | ARRIVAL TIMES ON RETURN |
|---|---|---|---|
| | pm | s d | am |
| ‡MANSFIELD TOWN | 1 52 | 10/6 | 3 15 |
| SUTTON JUNCTION | 1 59 | 10/6 | 3 9 |
| KIRKBY-IN-ASHFIELD East | 2 5 | 10/- | 3 4 |
| BURTON-ON-TRENT | 2 0 | 9/6 | 3 20 |
| †DERBY Midland | 2 22 | 9/- | 2 50 |
| BELPER | 2 36 | 8/6 | 2 35 |
| AMBERGATE | 2 50 | 8/3 | 2 26 |
| | | | |
| BLACKPOOL North ... arrive | pm 5 52 | Passengers return same day at | pm 10 55 |

† Derby Corporation 'buses will meet the return train on arrival at DERBY Midland Station to convey passengers along the various routes within the Borough boundary. Fares : Adults 1/4d., Children 8d. Passengers must obtain 'bus tickets at the time Rail tickets are obtained.

‡ Mansfield District Traction Company will provide transport to convey passengers from MANSFIELD TOWN STATION to HUTHWAITE, SKEGBY and other points on the Company's stage carriage routes. Fare : 1/- or 6d. according to distance. 'Bus tickets must be purchased from the Railway Booking Office before departure of the train.

CHILDREN under three years of age, free; three years and under fourteen, half-fare.

NOTICE AS TO CONDITIONS
These tickets are issued subject to the British Transport Commission's published Regulations and Conditions applicable to British Railways exhibited at their stations or obtainable free of charge at Station Booking Offices. For LUGGAGE ALLOWANCES also see those Regulations and Conditions.

RAIL TICKETS CAN BE OBTAINED IN ADVANCE AT STATIONS AND AGENCIES

Further information will be supplied on application to Stations, Official Railway Agents, or to W. B. CARTER, District Commercial Manager, DERBY. Telephone: Derby 42442, Extn. 204; or NOTTINGHAM Victoria. Telephone: Nottingham 44381, Extn. 32.

Travel in Rail Comfort

September 1955

BRITISH RAILWAYS

BR 35000

Arthur Gaunt & Sons (Printers) Ltd., Heanor, Derbyshire.

▲ There used to be excursions from all over the country to see the Illuminations. This leaflet promotes special trains from Derbyshire in 1955.

EXPRESS RESTAURANT CAR TRAINS
between KING'S CROSS & HARROGATE

# HARROGATE

## BRITAIN'S 100% SPA

ILLUSTRATED BROCHURE free on application to any G.N.R. Office or Superintendent of the Line, King's Cross Station, London, N.1.

# SOMETHING DIFFERENT

" *The only bad thing about a holiday is it is followed by a non-holiday.* "

Anonymous

# HEALTHFUL HOLIDAYS

BRITAIN IS RICHLY supplied with thermal springs, and the habit of visiting spas and taking the waters was widely practised in the late 18th century. In the Victorian era many spa towns became fashionable as holiday centres, and grand hotels offering all kinds of curative treatments were built. At the same time, the health-giving qualities of sea air were widely appreciated, encouraging the opening of numerous convalescent homes and hotels in or near traditional resort towns.

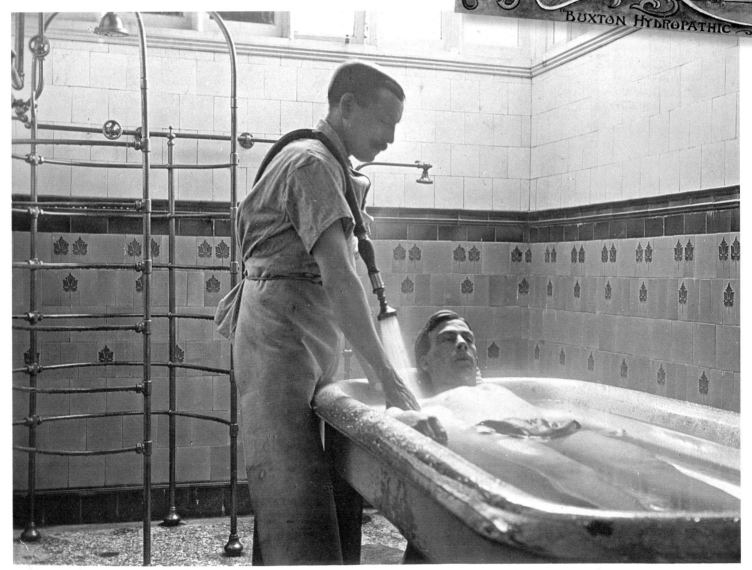

HUNTERS

**THE THERMAL BATHS, BUXTON**
(THE BUXTON DOUCHE-MASSAGE BATHS).

△ ◁ A spa town since Roman times, Buxton, in Derbyshire, began a new lease of life in the late 1700s. By the early 1900s several large hydropathic hotels, like those shown on these cards posted in 1909 and 1914, offered a wide range of treatments. The sender of the card to the left, describing his treatments, begins: 'This is the man who performed on me ...'

THE MINERAL WATER FOUNTAIN, BATH STREET, BATH

37551

△ The most famous Roman spa town in Britain is probably Bath, whose mineral waters have always been popular for both drinking and bathing. Here, in this 1930s card, two ladies take a break from their shopping to try the waters of the town's public fountain.

▷ This 1936 card of the Essex Convalescent Home at Clacton shows how the male and female inmates were strictly segregated.

LAWN OF PUMP HOUSE
LLANGAMMARCH WELLS.

LONDON & NORTH WESTERN RAILWAY COMPANY

△ An Edwardian scene of croquet on the Pump House lawn at Llangammarch Wells. This was one of a group of then popular spa towns in central Wales served by the London & North Western Railway, who published this card to encourage holiday traffic to the region.

CONVALESCENT

Essex Convalescent Home
Clacton on Sea

◁ Hydro hotels were popular at least until the 1950s. Here, a card posted in 1951 from Paignton, in Devon, shows a 1930s Art Deco extension to the town's original Victorian, tudor-style Hydro Hotel.

HYDRO HOTEL

TON HYDRO HOTEL.

No. 5. SITTING ROOM.—Victorian Convalescent Home for Surrey Women.

△◁ Many convalescent homes issued postcards for the use of residents. These two cards, from women's homes in Bognor Regis, Sussex, and in Hunstanton, Norfolk, date from the Edwardian period and the 1920s.

Hunstanton Convalescent Home (1), Hunstanton.

181

# SPECIAL INTERESTS

TRAVEL AGENTS, HOLIDAY ORGANIZATIONS and resorts have long appreciated the demand for holidays that cater for a specific clientele. This might include religious, philanthropic and temperance groups, orphanages and other institutions dedicated to the care of young people, and trades unions. Another part of this market catered for particular interests in a more general sense, for example holidays for older people or those mixing business and pleasure, and themed cruises.

△ Published in 1954 by the British Travel and Holidays Association, a forerunner of the BTA, this stylishly designed booklet is a gazetteer of places in Britain where work and play could be usefully combined.

△ This 1920s card shows happy children on holiday in Clacton, Essex. They were staying at a Sunday School Union home named after its late-Victorian benefactor, John Passmore Edwards.

▷ 'Other People's Children' is the caption on this card from Felixstowe, Suffolk, showing orphans and other children in care enjoying a holiday. Posted in 1912, the card has an intriguing message on the back, perhaps written by one of the carers: 'We shall have a women's exhibition next week. I don't know if it will be votes for women ...'

Felixstowe. "Other People's Children".

△ Many trades unions operated special holiday centres and holiday camps where their members could enjoy subsidized holidays. This 1960s card shows views of the NALGO Holiday Centre in the north of England.

▽ The temperance movement was very strong in late-Victorian and Edwardian Britain, and many seaside hotels followed strict temperance rules. Here, a group of residents, including a number of children, has gathered for a photograph on the steps of one such institution.

▷ Cruises have long catered for special interests. British India Line's *Dunera* ran educational cruises for children in the 1950s. The leaflet, issued in 1938, promotes a 'Music-Lovers' Cruise Party' in the Baltic on Canadian Pacific's *Montcalm*, with an orchestra, choir and music rooms.

△ The YMCA and the YWCA ran holiday centres in various parts of Britain. This 1950s view shows the elegant lounge and tea room at the Skegness Centre, complete with stage, Lloyd Loom furniture and tablecloths.

◁ ▷ ▽ Another trades union-run holiday camp was the Derbyshire Miners Holiday Centre at Rhyl, in North Wales, shown on this 1960s card. When coal mining was one of Britain's biggest industries, a number of mines took visitors on guided tours below ground. These photographs, taken at a mine in the 1950s, show a group of clean and smiling children about to make a visit down the mine, and the same group back on the surface, grimy, but still smiling.

DERBYSHIRE MINERS HOLIDAY CENTRE

**BOROUGH OF MARGATE**

*1857 - Centenary Year - 1957*

# OLD PEOPLE'S HOLIDAY

**11th MAY to 1st JUNE**

— and —

**14th to 28th SEPTEMBER**

A warm and friendly welcome is extended to all Old Age Pensioners to come to Sunny Margate in Centenary Year and enjoy the accommodation, entertainment and other amenities which have been arranged at greatly reduced rates during the scheme.

Organised by the Borough of Margate Publicity Committee in collaboration with the Margate Hotel and Boarding Association.

◁ In 1957 Margate, in Kent, celebrated its centenary by offering special cut-price holidays for old age pensioners, along with free use of deckchairs and putting green, and reduced-price tickets for theatres, cinemas, the winter gardens, coaches and taxis.

△ Another institution, the Holiday Home for Girls, was photographed in the 1920s somewhere on Britain's coast. The seated audience and the smartly dressed girls in the foreground suggest this was an open day, a sports day or some other special occasion.

**HOLIDAY FELLOWSHIP CENTRES IN GREAT BRITAIN**

● CENTRE
+ YOUTH CAMP

THE HOLIDA[...]

Marske by the S[...]

A Family Centre occupying an un[...] position, overlooking one of the finest stretches of sea and sand in the British Isles

To Mrs Finlay
61 Jesmond Park [...]
— Newcastle on Tyne

Greetings from W L Heppell

◁ The Holiday Fellowship is a Christian organization offering outdoor pursuits in the company of like-minded people. The map on this card from Marske by the Sea, in Yorkshire, shows the location of its holiday centres in 1955.

△ Another Christian institution that organized family holidays was the Methodist Guild. This is a group enjoying a week's holiday at the Guild's Eastbourne centre, in June 1950.

# FARM HOLIDAYS

DURING THE 19TH CENTURY much of Britain's population moved away from the country in search of work in the towns, and gradually rural life came to be viewed by urban dwellers as something of an idyll. An awareness of this, along with a growing interest in country pursuits and walking in particular, encouraged many farmers in the 1930s to begin offering bed and breakfast to holidaymakers. By the 1950s the concept of the farm holiday was well established as an essential area of diversification within agriculture.

BUSTABECK
FARM HOLIDAYS

◁ Haymaking and harvesting have always held a strong appeal for town and city dwellers. Here, in an Edwardian vision of an idyllic country life, twins have come to take a close look, providing a welcome break for the workers.

▽ In the 1920s five children from Bristol pose cheerfully for the camera, completely unfazed by the proximity of the cows. The caption says: 'Picnicking with dairy cows.'

△ By the 1960s, holidays that offered visitors the full farm experience had become popular. This card was sent from a Cumbrian farm whose owners had clearly taken on board the useful 'cash crop' that tourists represented.

## FULL ENGLISH BREAKFAST

The traditional English breakfast has long been a feature of a stay in a hotel or b&b. It all began in the Victorian era, when breakfast was a meal of extensive choice, generally laid out on the sideboard. There would be porridge and stewed fruit, then a huge range of cooked food simmering in chafing dishes – bacon, kidneys, sausages, kippers and other fish, potatoes, bubble and squeak. Often, cheeses and cold meats were also available. Breads, toast and muffins, with rich, dark marmalade, would round off the meal. By the 20th century the choice was more limited and the food was usually served at the table, but the 'full English' remains popular, with landladies and farmers' wives across the land priding themselves on the quality of their particular version.

The Original Cornish Kitchen Ware
Cornish Blue ⊚ T. G. Green

FISHING . SHOOTING . GOLFING . CARAVANNING . PONY RIDING

# FARM HOLIDAY

**GUIDE**

1958

BRITAIN'S BEST FARM AND COUNTRY HOUSES—COUNTY BY COUNTY

3/6

D BY ANGUS MACVICAR

◁ By 1958 this annual guide to farm holidays was a substantial publication, listing farms all over Britain that catered for visitors. Many gave urban dwellers the chance to take part in country sports.

▷ Farms that offered holidays usually had a few visitor-friendly animals, including bottle-fed lambs. The smartly dressed lady getting to know 'Tibby' was staying in a holiday bungalow on the farm.

◁ This young boy comes to terms with rural life in the form of a safely tethered and probably tame goat. In school cap and blazer and bursting out of his shorts and jumper, he could perhaps be a wartime evacuee sent 'on holiday' to the country.

▷ Coming face to face with large farm animals can be a frightening experience when you are not used to them. This duffle-coated small boy visiting a farm in the 1950s is clearly daunted, if not terrified, by the two huge horses looking down at him.

187

# OUR TOUR IN THE SCOTTISH HIGHLANDS – 1937

**①**

**③**

**②**

**④**

1. A GREY DAY AT CRIANLARICH, BUT THE SNOW ON THE MOUNTAINS BEYOND THE RAILWAY BRIDGE WAS VERY EXCITING.

2. TYPICAL HIGHLANDS SCENERY – SNOWY PEAKS AND A RIVER IN FULL SPATE.

3. A BRIEF STOP BESIDE LOCH TAY TO TAKE A PHOTOGRAPH.

4. LOCH LOMOND, WITH BEN LOMOND IN THE BACKGROUND. IT WAS RAINING HARD AND I REALLY DIDN'T WANT TO GET OUT OF THE AUSTIN!

**5**

**6**

**7**

5. LOCH LOMOND AGAIN, AND IT'S STILL COLD AND WET. I'M SO GLAD I BROUGHT THE FUR COAT WITH ME.

6. THE AUSTIN DWARFED BY THE BULK OF TAYMOUTH CASTLE.

7. JOURNEY'S END AND THE DRAMATIC SKYLINE OF STIRLING CASTLE — AND IT'S STILL RAINING!

# THE ISLE OF SKYE

SKYE'S LANDSCAPE of rocky peninsulas, moorland and cloud-capped mountains has attracted visitors at least since the Vikings. For centuries Skye was home to the MacLeods and the MacDonalds and, from the Victorian era and the start of regular ferry services from the mainland, their ancient clan traditions and castles have helped to inspire generations of holidaymakers.

Isle of Skye

## THE SLIGACHAN HOTEL

TARIFF AND GENERAL INFORMATION

Campbell's Hotel, Broadford. Under same Management.

▲ When the Sligachan Hotel published this brochure, a double room cost 10s 0d (50p) per night and table d'hôte dinner was 5s 0d (25p).

J. Arthur Dixon

▲ This 1970s guidebook promotes Skye's colourful landscape.

▶ A 1950s card shows the main ferry to Skye at that time, from Kyle of Lochalsh to Kyleakin.

► The Isle of Skye was widely claimed to be 'the rock-climbing centre par excellence of the British Isles'.

▼ Posted in 1963, this card shows one of the island's great mountains, Beinn na Caillich. The writer claims to have seen the Loch Ness Monster.

The Inaccessible Pinnacle, Skye.

Abraham's Series, Keswick Copyright.

► A typical 1950s day tour included the two ferry crossings, both of which had mainland rail connections, and a coach trip across Skye.

▼ Skye's tortuous coastline is apparent on this map card.

ISLE OF SKYE

MONDAYS, TUESDAYS, THURSDAYS and SATURDAYS All Year Round

TOUR No. 22

## SOUND OF SLEAT, MALLAIG AND ARMADALE (Isle of Skye) DAY TOUR

STEAMER FROM KYLE OF LOCHALSH TO ARMADALE VIA MALLAIG; MOTOR TO KYLEAKIN AND FERRY TO KYLE OF LOCHALSH

or the route may be reversed

TOUR FARE (SALOON) FROM KYLE OF LOCHALSH

17/6

e tickets are valid on the date for which issued and are obtainable only at
. MacBrayne's Office, Kyle of Lochalsh.

R STEAMER, MOTOR AND FERRY TIMES SEE OPPOSITE PAGE

88

## Guide to Isle of Skye

1/6

SCOTTISH YOUTH HOSTELS ASSOCIATION

ROYAL HOTEL

PORTREE, ISLE OF SKYE.

LOCH NEVIS ARRIVING AT PORTREE

PORTREE FROM SCORYBRECK

PORTREE FROM THE WEST

PORTREE FROM THE GOLF COURSE

B.7632.

◄ This 1968 YHA guide to Skye is full of useful information about the island and its history, along with details of the four hostels.

▲ The writer of this multiview card was staying in one of the best hotels in Skye's major town, Portree, in 1960.

from SAINT-GERVAIS to the VOZA PASS
by the MONT-BLANC RAILWAY

ROGER BRODERS

WINTER SPORTS
IN THE FRENCH ALPS

# GOING ABROAD

" *Never saw the sun shining so bright,*
*Never saw things going so right.* "

FROM 'BLUE SKIES',
BY IRVING BERLIN (1926)

# 'COME FLY WITH ME'

SCHEDULED PASSENGER FLIGHTS started after World War I, and by the 1930s a large network was in place, serving British destinations and much of western Europe. However, travel was expensive and aircraft were small and relatively slow. Even by 1939 few planes could carry more than 25 passengers. In World War II, aviation made huge advances, and in the 1950s, with the introduction of big, long-distance planes and then jet airliners, commercial flying really took off. By the 1960s, although business still dominated the market, holiday and pleasure traffic was beginning to grow exponentially, setting the pattern for the future.

△ In 1961, when this card was posted, London (Heathrow) Airport was an exciting place to visit. The message reads: 'Had a smashing journey down the M1. Stopped at Coventry to look at the new cathedral they are building. Have been watching the jets on the roof terrace at London Airport.'

◁ Even today, small, local airports have a certain appeal, but few could ever have matched the informality of St Mary's, on the Scilly Isles, as seen here in 1959.

△ Prior to the extension of the Piccadilly tube line to Heathrow, a scheduled bus service operated from a passenger terminal in Kensington, West London.

▷ Gatwick was re-developed as London's second airport from the early 1950s. By the 1960s it was noted for its modern, spacious elegance and the high quality of its signage.

◁ Silver City was famous in the 1950s and early 1960s for its scheduled cross-Channel flights carrying cars and their passengers. Here, in about 1959, a Bradford van is driven by its owner onto the Bristol freighter waiting on a Kent coast airfield.

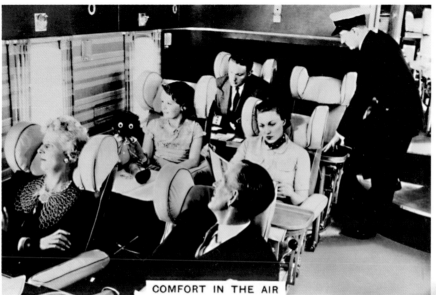

◁ In the 1930s Senior Service issued a set of cigarette cards entitled 'Flying'. This card shows the interior of an Empire flying boat, operated by Imperial Airways in the late 1930s. Comfort was to the fore, and the accommodation included a promenade deck, a smoking cabin and sleeping berths.

COMFORT IN THE AIR

▷ The Silver Wing service was operated by Imperial Airways between London and Paris in the late 1920s. This view of the passenger cabin in an Armstrong Whitworth Argosy airliner in service in 1927 is full of wonderful details: lights with flowery shades, curtains, open luggage racks, the drinks tray.

▽ Airline postcards were always popular. This shows a Vickers Viscount operated by Channel Airways on services from Southend, Ipswich and Portsmouth to Rotterdam, Paris, Ostend and the Channel Islands.

BEA takes you there and brings you back ✈ BRITISH EUROPEAN AIRWAYS ✈

**BEA**

fly

—for your holiday make it

**SCANDINAVIA**

BRITISH EUROPEAN AIRWAYS

**fly BEA**

YOUR FREE BAGGAGE ALLOWANCE

BRITISH EUROPEAN AIRWAYS

BRITISH EUROPEAN AIRWAYS "VIKING" CLASS AEROPLANE

△ After World War II, airlines had to rely initially on civil aircraft directly descended from RAF bombers. Typical was the Viking, seen here in the service of British European Airways in the 1950s, and derived from the famous wartime Wellington.

△◁ In 1946 BEA (British European Airways), a division of BOAC (British Overseas Airways Corporation), became a separate airline with responsibility for short-haul routes. It created its own style of publicity material. The 1957 baggage allowance leaflet above recommends ladies take 4 pairs of shoes, 1 suit, 2 frocks, 2 afternoon dresses, 2 evening dresses, 12 handkerchiefs, 1 hat, 2 pairs of gloves, but only 2 pairs of vests and panties.

# 'WE ARE SAILING'

THE DEVELOPMENT OF SCHEDULED shipping services across the Channel and the North Sea was linked directly to the expansion of the railway network. In the 1850s rival railway companies began to operate services from many ports on England's southern and eastern coasts, and competition was fierce. From the 1930s the carriage of cars became more important, leading to the emergence, from the 1950s, of the drive-on, drive-off vehicle carriers, which quickly came to dominate the market.

▽▷ These 1960s British Railways brochures give details of direct services between London and Paris for passengers and cross-Channel services for passengers with cars. Trains were scheduled to connect with dedicated ferry services across the Channel.

BRITISH RAILWAYS s.s. "DINARD"                1998

△ By the 1950s, when the SS *Dinard* came into service, cross-Channel ships were efficient, technically advanced and built for continuous service. She is seen here leaving Dover. Most ships now carried cars, but there were dedicated passenger vessels still in operation.

TAKE YOUR CAR
# H
## HARWICH
## HOOK OF HOLLAND

CARS · MOTOR CYCLES · CARAVANS · TRAILERS
*accompanied by passengers*

◁ This 1962 brochure promotes the day and night services then operated by British Railways between Harwich and the Hook of Holland. The journey time was around six hours, and the price for a return ticket for a car started at £10 plus £10 per passenger. There were 1st and 2nd class berths in shared cabins, and a few 'Cabins de Luxe', which were also available on day sailings.

Sealink
VALENCAY

◁ The Newhaven–Dieppe cross-Channel route was for decades an important link between London and Paris. Here, in the 1970s, the *Valencay*, a French car ferry operated jointly with Sealink, leaves Dieppe's old, city-centre harbour.

cross the channel
from Dover

LONDON
PARIS

Services
and
Fares

29 SEPTEMBER 1963 to 30 MAY 1964

BRITISH RAILWAYS

services and fares 1962
BRITISH & FRENCH RAILWAYS CAR FERRIES

△ British Railways introduced hovercrafts on short cross-Channel routes from 1966. These hybrid vessels offered much faster journey times, and the larger ones carried cars as well as passengers. From 1970 these services were marketed under the Seaspeed name. This promotional postcard depicts the car-carrying hovercraft *Princess Margaret*, which operated the Dover–Boulogne service.

◁△ Motor vehicles were carried on cross-Channel ferries from the early 1900s, but regular car-carrying services were not common until the 1930s. Before then, a limited number of cars could be carried on certain ships when 'accompanied by their passengers', as a 1927 leaflet promoting Southern Railway services from Southampton describes it. All vehicles were loaded by crane, the passengers having embarked on foot, and were generally stowed either in the hold or as deck cargo. This practice was maintained even when dedicated car-carrying ships came into service. These two photographs show this rather hazardous and time-consuming process under way in the 1930s and the 1950s.

# PACKAGE TOURS

THE ALL-INCLUSIVE HOLIDAY, given a new lease of life in the 1930s by coach companies, was greatly expanded in the 1950s. Road, rail and air services were all involved, but the airlines quickly came to dominate the business. By the 1960s the modern package tour was up and running, attracting many people who could never before have afforded holidays abroad. Hundreds of hotels were built, generally in the Mediterranean, frequently changing for ever the nature of hitherto unknown places.

▷ Package tours brought British holidaymakers into contact with new destinations and foreign traditions. Spain was always popular, with plenty of local colour.

△ Dan Air was one of the famous names of the package tour industry. Here, in the early 1980s, a girl steps off the plane into Ibizan sunshine, ready to enjoy to the full her family's first Continental holiday.

▷ This 1950s Sky Tours air and coach brochure hints at the style and elegance associated with early package tours, before the days of mass travel. A 'champagne luncheonette' was included in the price.

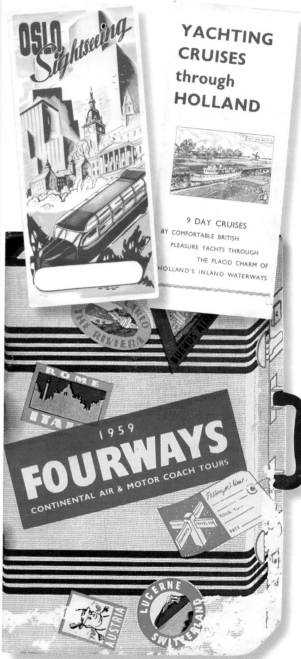

△ A number of British bus companies went into the package tour business in the 1950s, giving many people their first experience of the Continent. East Kent's 1959 brochure offered all-inclusive coach holidays in Holland, Germany, Switzerland, Austria, France, Italy and Denmark, at prices from £31 to £71 per person.

△ Fourways was more ambitious, offering in 1959 tours of Finland, Russia and Eastern Europe, along with the more usual European destinations. Several tours included Oslo, while others were even more adventurous, with yacht holidays in Holland and elsewhere. Prices for tours in the leaflet shown here started at 30 guineas (£31.50).

# A TRIP TO PARIS

LONG REGARDED as a city of romance, Paris has for over a century been a special destination for short visits. From the late 1800s dedicated rail and cross-Channel services linked London and Paris. Direct flights began in the 1920s, and by the 1960s rail and air combined to speed up the journey. At the same time all-inclusive packages and weekend breaks became more popular.

▷ Restaurants, and enticing menus, were part of the appeal for British visitors used to postwar rationing and indifferent food. This delightful pen-and-watercolour menu dates from the 1930s and for someone must have been a charming souvenir of a memorable occasion.

△ The classic Paris multiview card was ever popular. This is a 1950s example.

△ There's always time for a quick coffee in a backstreet bar. Here, it is sunny enough to sit outside, on the metal café chairs. Behind, the simple façade, with its lacy curtain and classic adverts for Ricard and Pastis, is typical of innumerable Parisian neighbourhood bars.

▷ The Silver Arrow was a London–Paris rail–air link during the 1960s, a short-lived example of British Railways responding to the growing challenge of air travel.

△ No visit to Paris was complete without a night at the Moulin Rouge.

▷ For well over a century the Eiffel Tower has been the icon of the city, and posting a card from the top has been a perennially popular activity with many visitors, including the sender of this particular example.

◁ The magic of Paris had a universal appeal, and many British came on package tours. This 1950s group was photographed at Versailles.

△ Every visitor needs a map, and basic ones such as this were given away by hotels.

# IN THE MOUNTAINS

The lure of the mountains dates back to the late 19th century and by the Edwardian period winter sports were well established as holiday activities, thanks in part to spreading railway networks. The Alps were the favourite destination, but the Dolomites and the Pyrenees were also popular. In the 1920s steady improvements in roads increased the appeal of mountain landscapes to cyclists and motorists in the summer months, while, at the same time, developing mountain resorts broadened their appeal by attracting walkers. After World War II, skiing grew hugely in popularity.

▷▽ Touring the Pyrenees on a tandem was no mean feat in the 1930s, but this couple seem remarkably relaxed about it all. The Col du Tourmalet is one of the highest of the passes and has featured on the Tour de France.

◁ Mountain railways made many of the Swiss Alpine peaks accessible to ordinary tourists. Typical was the line up to the 1900m (6,200ft) summit of the Stanserhorn, high above Lake Lucerne. It had its own hotel, to allow visitors to enjoy the magnificent Alpine panoramas at sunrise and sunset, as described in this 1930s leaflet.

▷ Local guides were readily available for any visitors wanting individual walking tours in the mountains. For this Edwardian couple, and perhaps a friend taking the photograph, there is safety in numbers: they have three guides.

◁ For summer visitors the mountains offered sunshine, wonderful views and wild flowers, along with an extensive network of hostels, hotels and chalets.

▷ The moment of triumph: in this 1930s photograph, a local guide offers his congratulations to the English climber he has led safely to the top.

SCHWEIZERHOF
LUCERNE

◁▽ Despite somewhat primitive roads, exploring the mountain regions of Europe was increasingly popular from the 1920s. In the main photograph, British holidaymakers in the late 1930s have stopped on a mountain track to enjoy the spectacular view. Inset below are pictures of another family doing a similar thing in the 1950s, by which time cars and roads had improved considerably.

△ In a Continental mountain resort some time in the Edwardian era, these skaters have paused on the ice for a group photograph.

HAPPY DAYS IN AUSTRIA

With every Good Wish for Christmas and the New Year

E.MARTIN

◁ Comic and glamour cards were not confined to the seaside, and there are plenty with mountain and winter sports themes. These two postcards, both produced for British visitors, are typical.

▷ Posing in a glorious setting, this 1950s group cheerfully shows off what was then the latest thing in ski wear.

◁ Posted in Bournemouth in 1907, this card describes 'an adventurous time in the Bernese Oberland' enjoyed by a British family. Here they all stand, with their guide, in the snow, wearing rather amazing hats. The message on the back is: 'I am "hors de combat", but the wife and family are fit as fiddles.'

▷ In the late 1950s and early 1960s the SNCF, the French railway network, produced a series of stylish guides to various regions of France, designed to encourage the British holiday trade. This one, with its striking cover designed by Guy Georget, was issued in 1960.

**FRANCE**
THE FRENCH ALPS

FRENCH RAILWAYS

# CRUISING

CRUISING GOES BACK to the late 1800s, with small, comfortably equipped ships inspired by royal yachts. In the 1920s the habit became more established, and routes were offered in many parts of the world, often in the winter, on ships withdrawn from transatlantic services. The first large ships dedicated to cruising went into service in the 1930s, operated by famous names such as P&O, Cunard and Canadian Pacific. In the 1950s cruising holidays really caught on, and more and more companies entered the field. Today, dedicated cruise ships get ever larger and more luxurious, while smaller, and sometimes older, ships ensure that cruising can appeal to all levels of the market.

▷▽ Cunard's *QE2* set new standards for both cruising and transatlantic routes. A classic souvenir was the envelope posted on board the preview cruise in April 1969, but for most people a luggage label had to suffice.

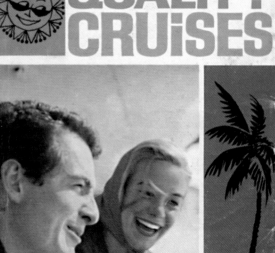

△ This 1930s card of the Cunarder *Ascania*, posted before the ship had even set sail, says: 'It seems to be a delightful boat & we are going to have a good trip.' Many people are inspired to go on a cruise by friends.

▷ The first thing to do when choosing a cruise is to collect the brochures. This is a Cunard one from 1964/65, and it is seductively filled with photographs of ship life. Then, in the pre-*QE2* era, the principal ships were the old *Queen Mary* and the *Mauretania*, and cruises included the Atlantic islands, the West Indies and the Mediterranean.

▷ ▽ P&O has long been another great cruising name, and their brochures have always been stylish, informative and rich in delightful period detail. Typical is the checklist of 1939 cruises (below, inset), with the names of some of the most famous cruise liners of that era. Even more appealing is the classic design of the 1952 brochure for the *Himalaya*, another well-known liner, while nothing could be more 1960s than the cover of their 1968 'Sunshine Holiday Cruises' brochure.

Summer Cruises
'HIMALAYA'
Shore Excursions
1952 P&O

P&O
40 Sunshine Holiday Cruises 1968

1939
P&O
CRUISES
TO THE MEDITERRANEAN
W. AFRICA · ATLANTIC IS.
NORWEGIAN FJORDS
NORTHERN CAPITALS

VICEROY OF INDIA
STRATHNAVER
STRATHMORE
STRATHEDEN
STRATHALLAN

Revised issue dated Jan

◁ *Canberra*, one of the most iconic ships of her era, entered service in 1961. Large, fast, stylish and decidedly modern, she was enjoyed by thousands of cruisers during her active life of over 35 years with P&O.

▽ Postcards reveal how closely linked the decor of cruise ships is to contemporary style. This shows the 1st Class Verandah Café on the *Himalaya*, with its 1950s period textiles, lighting and woodgrain wall finishes.

P. & O. HIMALAYA    1st CLASS VERANDAH CAFE

QUEEN MARY

YOU ENJOY THE BEST

◁ The cruise really starts with the journey to the embarkation port. This picture shows a group of passengers on the quay in Southampton, lining up to board the White Star liner *Doric* in the late 1920s.

WHITE STAR LINE RMS DORIC

*Cunard*
# PROGRAMME
## for
# TODAY

D. TOURS

P. & O.
"STRATHMORE."

TUESDAY,
27TH JULY, 1937

Fujiyama, Japan

## BREAKFAST

TEA        COFFEE        COCOA

APPLES      GRAPE FRUIT     ORANGES

PRESERVED GREEN FIGS WITH CREAM
STEWED GOOSEBERRIES WITH RICE

CORN FLAKES   SHREDDED WHEAT   GRAPE NUTS   FORCE
OATMEAL PORAGE   ROLLED OATS

GRILLED HALIBUT
TO ORDER  KIPPERED HERRINGS        YARMOUTH BLOATERS
SMOKED HADDOCK

FRIED WILTSHIRE BACON

                    1          2          3          4
EGGS    FRIED    POACHED   TURNED   SCRAMBLED
To Order

             1          2          3          4
OMELETS   PLAIN   KIDNEY   SAVOURY   HAM

GRILLED CUMBERLAND HAM        PORK SAUSAGES
CHOPS       STEAKS          BAKED TOMATOES

POTATOES   CREAMED   SARATOGA   MACAIRE

CURRANT SCONES   TOAST   CREAM SCONES   CROISSANTS
FRENCH BATONS   BREAKFAST ROLLS   WHITE & BROWN BREAD
OATCAKES       RUSKS      PULLED BREAD

COLD SIDEBOARD
YORK HAM      ROAST LAMB      OX TONGUE

MARMALADE     HONEY    JAMS     GOLDEN SYRUP

"MAURETANIA'S" GRAND HALL

SUITE ROOM

RYTHING

△ Promotional postcards are often given away to passengers in their cabins. This 1960s example promotes Christmas cruising, a popular way to escape and enjoy some winter sun. It illustrates many aspects of life on board the famous *Queen Mary*. A day on a cruise ship is packed with activities and there is always too much to do. So, after a large and leisurely breakfast, passengers begin with a look at the daily programme to see what is on offer – perhaps deck quoits, bridge, a lecture, ballroom dancing or some napkin folding.

BATHERS
PLEASE DO NOT USE THESE
CHAIRS WITHOUT WRAPS

THERS
DO NOT USE THESE
WITHOUT WRAPS

◁△ Everyone likes to have photographs to take home, and every cruise ship has its resident photographer to record the highlights of the cruise. Edward and Elsie were captured on deck, just settling into their cruise on the *Arandora Star* in 1935.

◁ The ship, a 1930s cruise liner, has anchored in some exotic spot, and this lady has dressed smartly, ready to go ashore.

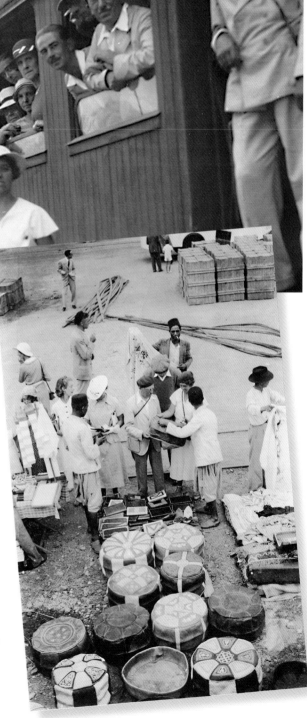

△▷ The shore excursions are an important part of any cruise. Above: most outings are by coach but here, somewhere in Europe in the 1930s, the trip is on a train, which has been shunted onto a quayside siding right next to the ship. Right: the highlight of any shore excursion is the opportunity to shop. Here, some passengers, perhaps in Egypt or North Africa, are haggling with the quayside vendors selling leather goods.

◁ These jolly folk are enjoying the sun on the deck. It is in the 1930s, with dress styles decidedly casual. The clutter on the deck, and the deckchairs, suggest that this was probably not a very expensive cruise.

◁ The traditional maritime ceremony of Crossing the Line is still practised on many cruise ships when they cross the Equator. This 1920s picture shows all the traditional characters involved in the high jinks, including Neptune and his lovely attendants, the barber, the doctor and Britannia.

▷ Many shipping lines were adventurous with their menus, frequently commissioning designs from well-known artists and illustrators. This dashing mermaid was drawn in 1955 for the Orient Line's *Orion* by Derek Dekk.

◁△ Dining is an important ritual, and every cruise has formal and gala dinners. As this group on the *Queen Mary* shows, these are a stalking ground for the ship's photographer. And there are always the commemorative menus. The one shown above is from the *Circassia*, in the Mediterranean in 1963, and typically is signed on the back by all members of the table party.

213

# OUR TRIP TO THE NETHERLANDS – 1953

❶

❷ ❸

1. We flew from Croydon to Schiphol, the airport for Amsterdam. It was a bit bumpy and noisy in the Dakota, but we soon recovered.

2. The weather was lovely – just right for exploring Amsterdam.

3. The hotel was very friendly and they looked after us well, especially Bob the poodle.

4

5

6

4. THE GIRLS COULDN'T RESIST TRYING ON A PAIR OF KLOMPEN!

5. A DIP IN THE SEA AT ZANDVOORT – QUITE A PLACE.

6. TIME FOR A NICE POT OF TEA BEFORE LEAVING FOR THE AIRPORT.

# FRANCE

IN THE EARLY 20TH CENTURY it became very fashionable for wealthy Britons to holiday in France, especially in the Mediterranean and the mountain regions. Also popular were northern resorts such as Dieppe and Le Touquet. However, for the majority, French holidays remained a dream until the 1950s and 1960s, when wider car ownership, improved ferry services and better trains made France much more accessible.

◄▼ Dieppe was always popular with the British. The 1902 cycling guide was printed in Britain, and the postcard is from the same era, when French stamps had to be on the front.

► The French tourist board was efficient at promoting the attractions of the country. This is a regional guide, dated 1957, to Languedoc and the Cévennes.

▼ Ever popular is the telegram or lazy postcard. The original buyer of this 1950s version, however, was too lazy to write it.

*Pneu* **MICHELIN**

Guide

## PROVENCE

avec carte touristique

Le Pont du Gard *(D'après photo Yvon, Paris.)*

**1948**  Services de Tourisme  le guide et la carte: 180 fr.
MICHELIN
97 Bᵉ Pereire, Paris 17ᵉ·Tél.: Carnot 64.00

*Cycle Rides ·· around Dieppe.*

BY

OCTAVIUS C. STONE,
F.R.G.S.

1902

SIXPENCE.

◄ Few British travellers set foot in France without their green Michelin guide.

FRANCE
LANGUEDOC / ROUSSILLON
ROUERGUE / GÉVAUDAN
CÉVENNES
1957

hôtels prix tout compris
prices all inclusive
hôtels volle pension

AU BORD

TÉLÉGRAMME VACANCES

| ORIGINE | DATE: | MOTIF |

AU BORD DE LA MER - VACANCES - PAS LE TE... D'ÉCRI...
VACANCES SENSAS' - PAYS AS' TAP...
GENS BOUL D'AS, APPÉTIT DU TONN'
TEMPS FORMID' - MILLE BECOTS -

MARINE

CAMPING

LA MER HOULEUSE

BORD DE PLAGE

SUR LA CÔTE

LE FLOT QUI MONTE

◀ The distinctive graphic style used by the French tourist board in the 1950s is illustrated in this 1955 guide to the Pyrenees.

▶ A 1930s card promotes the Hôtel Moderne in Barfleur, a little resort town on the Normandy coast. The hotel was famous for its food.

BARFLEUR (Manche)

HOTEL MODERNE, près de la Gare, titulaire pour sa Bonne Cuisine de 9 premiers prix (1923 à 1931) et de la 1re Médaille d'Or aux Concours de l'Automobile-Club de l'Ouest.

HOTEL RESTAURANT MODERNE

GRAND PRIX DE LA BONNE CUISINE À LA SALLE NORMANDE RENDEZ-VOUS DES FINS GOURMETS

LES ALPES

la savoie
le dauphiné
la côte d'azur

ROB DAC 1926

EN CARS PLM

offert par les établissements
REPELLIN ET TRAFFORT 6 PLACE GRENETTE GRENOBLE
téléph: 10-71 et 0-45 ■■■ télégraphe: ERTA GRENOBLE

ALSACE
VOSGES JURA
FRANCE

J. JACQUELIN

FRENCH RAILWAYS

48 CANNES
Iles de Lerins - St-Honorat, l'ancien Château

▲ A typical card of the 1920s, printed in the dramatic colours associated with Mediterranean resorts such as Cannes.

▲ Exploring by bus was easy in the 1920s, when this brochure was issued to promote tours operated by the famous PLM (Paris, Lyon, Méditerranée) railway.

▶ SNCF, French Railways, produced this series of brochures with colourful, avant-garde covers in the 1950s.

# LUGGAGE LABELS

**G^d· HOTEL COSMOPOLITE · BRUXELLES**

COSMOPOLITE

HOTEL B

VENEZIA

BAUER
GRÜNWALD

LNER

**NORTH BRITISH STATION**

TELEPHONES:
CENTRAL
8966 to 8972

PASSENGERS FROM LONDON
(Waverley Station), via THE E
DEPART FROM KING'S CROS
BY THE MIDLAND RAILWAY
ST. PANCRAS STATIO

TELEGRAMS:
"BRITISH"
EDINBURGH

## EDINBURGH.

THE HOTEL IS IN DIRECT COMMUNICATION WITH WAVERLEY STATION
BY ELECTRIC LIFTS, AND THE HOTEL PORTERS ATTEND THE ARRIVAL
OF ALL TRAINS.
ALL COMMUNICATIONS TO BE ADDRESSED TO THE HOTEL "MANAGER."

McC. & Co. Ltd.

BR 21752

BRITISH RAILWAYS - SOUTHERN REGN.

## RESERVED
### SEAT

PENALTY under Bye-Law 18 for UNAUTHORISED
REMOVAL of this LABEL—£5.

FIRENZE

GRAND HOTEL
MEDITERRANEO

NORTH EASTERN RAILWAY.

**From YORK.**

## Lowestoft

(G. E.)

Southern Railway.    STOCK. 787 DD

(8/28)

From _____   TO

## GUERNSEY

BADEN-

GRAND HOTEL

GEORGES V

OSTENDE
BELGIQUE

HÔTEL
ADELPHI
PARIS

HOTEL
ESPLENDIDO

PUERTO DE SOLLER-MALLORCA

LEVUE

ADEN

HOTEL
CONTINENTAL
BASEL

HOTEL
ACCADEMIA
VERONA
ITALIA.

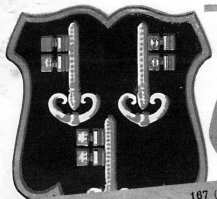

# INDEX

**Postcard 1 (top left)**

VALENTINE'S SERIES

POST CARD

FAMOUS THROUGHOUT THE WORLD

Correspondence. MC

Printed in Great Britain.

SHERINGHAM. R.S.O. 12.30 PM JL 23 NORFOLK

"Here is a P.C.
for your Collection.
You will soon
Have me Back again
yours
Auth

Miss N. Hall
C/o R.B. Jaconbtz
Ewell House
Ewell
Surrey

**Postcard 2 (top right)**

Dear nanny
We are having a
nice time here. We
went to the Zoo
yesterday. And then
we went on the
beach. Going to see
the lights tonight.
Love from us all
Angela. x x x x x

HOPE EVERYTHING IS
GOING ALRIGHT. SEE YOU
PONTIN'S BLACKPOOL HOLIDAY CAMP, SITT.
LYTHAM ST. ANNES, LANCASHIRE    R5628

Photo Precision Limited, St. Ives, Huntingdon.

BLACKPOOL FYLDE 5 PM 23 OCT 1978 LANCS

REMEMBER to use the POST CODE

Mrs W. EDWARDS
c/o WYNDEE KENNE
ABERGAVENNY
BLAENAVO
GWEN
S. WAL

**Postcard 3 (middle left)**

CHRISTCHURCH 19 MAY 1970 HANTS.

Dear Mrs Hinch
Got here safe the weather
not to bad good food and
Bed. Hope you all are quite
well. It is a bit Lonly on
ones own. See you soon
Mrs Stenard

PRINTED IN GREAT BRITAIN

THE MINIATURE RAILWAY, CHRISTCHURCH    PT2901

Mrs G Hinch
34 Grotto Road
Weybridge
Surrey.

**Postcard 4 (middle right)**

13. 9. 38.

POST CARD

CORRESPONDENCE

Where we are staying
is close to the Lighthouse
on the top of the cliffs
& the views are beautiful.
Delightful weather
& a good holiday.
Kind regards
G. R. Stern

Published by C. Munday & Co., Church Square, Cromer.

— THIS IS A REAL PHOTOGRAPH —

CROMER 4.45 PM 13 SEP 1938 NORFOLK

ADDRESS ONLY

Miss D. Lambert
46 Alexandra
Botley
Oxford

**Postcard 5 (bottom left)**

POST CARD

FOR COMMUNICATION    ADDRESS

THIS IS A REAL PHOTOGRAPH

Published by J. P. Dewar, The Square, Port William.

monreith, Wigtownshire
Sept. 8th

Many thanks for your having
communications which I
haven't been very good at
answering! I'm so glad you were
of getting abroad & I hope it has
been fine. The children & I all
indulged in mumps at his Gate
but only lightly thank goodness.
Nouddie & I are having a lovely
holiday in Scotland, & return
home next Sunday.
Much love from
Hope.

Miss Mary Wall.
75 Hornsey Lane Gdns.
Highgate.
N. London. N.6.

**Postcard 6 (bottom right)**

POST CARD

PRINTED IN GREAT BRITAIN

For INLAND Postage only this
space may be used for communication.

The Address only to be written
here.

Valentine's Series

HARROGATE

Kind regards
to all you know
I know

Arthur Newton

Miss N. Doman
233 Oxford Rd
Manchester

## Postcard 1 (top left)

Post Card.

This space may be used for communication

London 13-8-08

Chère Maria

Superbe cette Exposition

Henri

Madame Forissier
11. Rue Robert
S'Etienne
(France) (Loire)

## Postcard 2 (top right)

POST CARD.

THIS SPACE MAY BE USED FOR INLAND COMMUNICATION POST CARD RATE, AND FOR FOREIGN AT LETTER RATE.

THE ADDRESS ONLY TO BE WRITTEN HERE.

Dear Miss Prescott

Tell you brothers I will call this Evening (Wed.) Hoping to find you in. I will bring my card book with me. Hoping you are all well.

Yours Reggie

(ss)

Miss Prescott
268 Upper Parliament s
Liverpool

## Postcard 3 (middle left)

S.S. "AUSTRALIS" — CHANDRIS LINES
The largest one class liner in the world. Completely air-conditioned, spacious and distinctively designed public rooms and cabins.
Length 723 ft.- Speed 22 knots - Displacement 35,400 tons. Accommodates 2,000 passengers, all in One Class.
Orient & Pacific Cruises.
Regular Service U.K. — GREECE — AUSTRALIA — NEW ZEALAND.

ESPANA 5 PTAS CORREOS

arrived on board last ... we have had very ... weather, right from ... thampton. People are ... sick everywhere. So far ... been lucky. Haven't ... my luggage, but cabin ... is on deck as I've seen ... one. I keep getting lost ... the ship. Hope you are both ... love Pat

Mr. & Mrs. J. Howie,
80, Moss Heights Ave. (9/R),
Cardonald,
Glasgow, G52 2TY,
Scotland,
U.K.

## Postcard 4 (middle right)

POST CARD.

PEACOCK BRAND TRADE MARK

"PEACOCK" SERIES.

This space may also be used for communication in the United Kingdom only.

FOR THE ADDRESS ONLY.

Miss B. Pointer
Brook
nr. Lyndhurst
Hants

## Postcard 5 (bottom left)

POST CARD

THE ADDRESS ONLY TO BE WRITTEN HERE

ONE PENNY

Batavia Zoo
Sent to sis.

S.A.H.

Miss H. Little
9 Stanhope Gardens
London S.W. 7

## Postcard 6 (bottom right)

POST CARD

DENNIS Productions

3d INTERNATIONAL BOTANICAL CONGRESS

Miss M. Wright.
Hope House.
High Legh
Nr. Knutsford
Cheshire

Newcolour

W 0752

# Author's Acknowledgements

Some years ago I began to amass photographs and ephemera relating to holidays, partly because it seemed to be a subject that reflected a universal experience and partly because no one else appeared to be bothering with such vital and lively material. I hoped it would lead to a book, and a chance to celebrate and commemorate the hundreds of anonymous photographs and thousands of equally unknown people they had captured through much of the 20th century. Now it is done, I want to thank those who have made it possible. First, the many dealers and enthusiasts at postcard and antiques fairs, and on the internet, who have sold me interesting things; secondly, Mic Cady and AA Publishing, who have made it possible; thirdly, the designer, Dawn Terrey, who has brought the idea to life; fourthly, Sue Gordon, my brilliant editor, and fellow enthusiast, without whom nothing much would have happened; and fifthly, my wife Chrissie, who not only has had to live with me, the idea and all the material that has poured into the house while remaining, as ever, totally tolerant and supportive, but who also chose to scan every image in the book. Now she needs a holiday.

# Picture Credits

The illustrations in this book are comprised mainly of amateur photographs, supported by postcards and printed ephemera of many kinds. Photographs have been selected from family albums or have been acquired on the open market via fairs or the internet. All the usual processes to identify photographers and copyright holders have been applied, but by their nature amateur and family photographers are normally anonymous. If readers can identify the people in the pictures or the photographers who took them, the author and the publishers would be delighted to hear from them.

The illustrations, unless stated otherwise, have come from the author's collection. For the loan of other images, the author is very grateful to Bonham and Phyl Bazeley, Peter Cove, Jeanne Darrington, Sue Gordon, Joan Gurney, Alison Lubbock and Anne Scott.

The author and publishers are also grateful to Tony Price at www.lordprice.co.uk for the use of images on the following pages: 7, 18 left, 19 right, 33 ,61, 77, 93 top right, 101, 149, 179, 193.

Author, Paul Atterbury, on holiday on the Norfolk coast in 1951.

Managing Editor, Sue Gordon, with her younger sister, on holiday in Swanage, Dorset, in 1955.

Art Editor, Dawn Terrey, on holiday on Winchelsea beach, East Sussex, in 1976.